# Low Carb, High Protein Cookbook
## 100+ Recipes for Weight Loss and Muscle Gain
## Simple, Delicious Meals for Energy and Fat Loss

By
Ethan White

**Copyright © 2025 by Ethan White**

All rights reserved. No part of this book may be reproduced, distributed, or transmitted in any form or by any means, electronic or mechanical, including photocopying, recording, or any information storage or retrieval system, without prior written permission from the author, except for brief quotations used in reviews or scholarly articles.

# Table of contents

## WELCOME TO YOUR HIGH-PROTEIN, LOW-CARB JOURNEY ............... 7
- What is the High-Protein, Low-Carb Diet? ............... 7
- Why Choose a High-Protein, Low-Carb Diet? ............... 7
- How Does This Diet Work? ............... 8
- The Science behind Protein and Carbs ............... 8
- Key Benefits of the High-Protein, Low-Carb Approach ............... 8
- How to Use This Cookbook ............... 9
- How to Get Started ............... 9

## CHAPTER 1: ............... 10

## HIGH-PROTEIN, LOW-CARB DIET BASICS ............... 10
- The Essentials of a High-Protein, Low-Carb Diet ............... 10
- Understanding Macronutrients ............... 10
- What Are Proteins, Fats, and Carbs? ............... 10
- The Role of Each Macronutrient in Your Body ............... 11
- How the High-Protein, Low-Carb Diet Works ............... 11
- The Process of Ketosis and Fat-Burning ............... 12
- Why Protein is Important ............... 12
- How Carbs Affect Your Body ............... 12
- The Truth Behind Low-Carb Eating ............... 12
- Foods to Embrace and Foods to Avoid ............... 13
- Foods to Cut Back On or Eliminate ............... 13

## CHAPTER 2: ............... 14

## BREAKFAST RECIPES ............... 14
- Overview of a High-Protein Breakfast ............... 14
- 1. Spinach and Mushroom Scrambled Eggs ............... 14
- 2. Greek Yogurt with Mixed Berries and Almonds ............... 15
- 3. Chia Seed Pudding with Coconut Milk ............... 15
- 4. Egg Muffins with Bacon and Spinach ............... 16
- 5. Protein Pancakes with Sugar-Free Syrup ............... 16
- 6. Avocado and Egg Breakfast Bowl ............... 17
- 7. Cottage Cheese and Cucumber Salad ............... 17
- 8. Almond Flour Banana Bread (Sugar-Free) ............... 18
- 9. Zucchini and Feta Omelet ............... 18
- 10. Cinnamon Flaxseed Porridge ............... 19
- 11. Peanut Butter Chia Smoothie ............... 19
- 12. Low-Carb Protein Oats ............... 20
- 13. Cottage Cheese and Chive Breakfast Bowl ............... 21
- 14. Smoked Salmon and Avocado Breakfast Bowl ............... 21
- 15. Protein-Packed Smoothie Bowl ............... 22
- 16. Avocado, Bacon, and Egg Breakfast Cups ............... 22
- 17. Low-Carb Egg and Veggie Scramble ............... 23
- 18. Almond Flour Pancakes with Greek Yogurt ............... 23
- 19. Tofu Scramble with Veggies ............... 24
- 20. Protein-Packed Smoothie ............... 24

## CHAPTER 3: LUNCH RECIPES ............... 26
- Overview of a High-Protein Lunch ............... 26
- 1. Grilled Chicken and Avocado Salad ............... 26
- 2. Tuna Salad Lettuce Wraps ............... 26
- 3. Turkey and Veggie Lettuce Cups ............... 27

- 4. Zucchini Noodles with Grilled Chicken ... 28
- 5. Egg Salad with Avocado and Mustard Dressing ... 28
- 6. Spicy Grilled Salmon with a Side of Cabbage Slaw ... 29
- 7. Lentil and Quinoa Salad with Feta Cheese ... 29
- 8. Low-Carb Turkey Meatballs with Zoodles ... 30
- 9. Grilled Steak with Spinach and Mushrooms ... 31
- 10. Broccoli and Cheese Stuffed Chicken Breast ... 31
- 11. Grilled Shrimp Salad with Lemon Vinaigrette ... 32
- 12. Chicken and Broccoli Stir-Fry ... 32
- 13. Spicy Chicken Lettuce Wraps ... 33
- 14. Grilled Turkey and Cheese Lettuce Wraps ... 34
- 15. Cauliflower Rice Stir-Fry with Chicken ... 34
- 16. Avocado Tuna Salad ... 35
- 17. Grilled Portobello Mushroom with Spinach and Cheese ... 35
- 18. Chicken Caesar Salad (Without the Croutons) ... 36
- 19. Grilled Chicken and Pesto Zoodles ... 37
- 20. Beef and Vegetable Stir-Fry ... 37
- 21. Chicken, Cucumber, and Hummus Bowl ... 38
- 22. Shrimp and Avocado Salad with Lime Dressing ... 38
- 23. Baked Salmon with Asparagus and Lemon ... 39
- 24. Chicken and Avocado Lettuce Wraps ... 39
- 25. Cauliflower Rice and Chicken Stir-Fry ... 40

## CHAPTER 4: DINNER RECIPES ... 41

- 1. Baked Salmon with Lemon and Asparagus ... 41
- 2. Chicken and Veggie Stir-Fry with Soy Sauce ... 41
- 3. Grilled Steak with Garlic Butter and Veggies ... 42
- 4. Stuffed Bell Peppers with Ground Turkey ... 43
- 5. Cauliflower Rice with Shrimp ... 43
- 6. Zucchini Lasagna with Ground Beef ... 44
- 7. Cilantro-Lime Chicken with Roasted Vegetables ... 45
- 8. Grilled Shrimp Skewers with Cauliflower Rice ... 45
- 9. Spaghetti Squash with Marinara and Turkey Meatballs ... 46
- 10. Grilled Portobello Mushrooms with Goat Cheese ... 47
- 11. Lemon Herb Chicken with Roasted Brussels Sprouts ... 47
- 12. Baked Cod with Roasted Vegetables ... 48
- 13. Chicken and Spinach Stuffed Sweet Potatoes ... 49
- 14. Eggplant Parmesan (Low-Carb Version) ... 49
- 15. Beef and Broccoli Stir-Fry ... 50
- 16. Spicy Baked Chicken with Avocado Salsa ... 51
- 17. Grilled Chicken and Cucumber Salad ... 51
- 18. Roasted Lemon Herb Chicken with Green Beans ... 52
- 19. Grilled Pork Chops with Brussels Sprouts ... 53
- 20. Eggplant and Ground Turkey Stir-Fry ... 53
- 21. Baked Chicken Thighs with Cauliflower Mash ... 54

## CHAPTER 5: SNACKS & SIDES ... 55

- Overview of High-Protein, Low-Carb Snacks ... 55
- 1. Hard-Boiled Eggs with Salt and Pepper ... 55
- 2. Crispy Roasted Chickpeas ... 55
- 3. Avocado and Tuna Bites ... 56
- 4. Greek Yogurt with Flaxseeds and Almonds ... 56
- 5. Cheese and Cucumber Bites ... 57
- 6. Roasted Almonds with Sea Salt ... 57
- 7. Veggie Sticks with Hummus ... 58
- 8. Roasted Pumpkin Seeds ... 58
- 9. Cheese-Stuffed Olives ... 59
- 10. Mini Quinoa Bites ... 59

11. Edamame with Sea Salt .................................................................................................. 59
12. Guacamole with Veggie Chips ....................................................................................... 60
13. Cottage Cheese and Cherry Tomato Bowl ................................................................... 60
14. Smoked Salmon and Cream Cheese Rolls .................................................................. 61
15. Turkey and Cheese Roll-Ups ........................................................................................ 61
16. Veggie Frittata Bites ....................................................................................................... 62
17. Cucumber and Hummus Bites ...................................................................................... 62
18. Almond Butter Celery Sticks ......................................................................................... 63
19. Mini Cucumber and Cheese Bites ................................................................................ 63
20. Turkey Avocado Roll-Ups .............................................................................................. 64

## CHAPTER 6: DESSERTS .................................................................................................. 65

1. Coconut Macaroons ........................................................................................................ 65
2. Chocolate Protein Balls .................................................................................................. 65
3. Sugar-Free Almond Flour Cookies ................................................................................ 66
4. Avocado Chocolate Mousse ........................................................................................... 67
5. Low-Carb Cheesecake Bites .......................................................................................... 67
6. Peanut Butter Protein Bars ............................................................................................. 68
7. Berry Chia Pudding ......................................................................................................... 68
8. Keto-Friendly Chocolate Cupcakes ............................................................................... 69
9. Almond Flour Cake with Cream Cheese Frosting ...................................................... 69
10. Baked Apple Cinnamon Protein Bars ......................................................................... 70
11. Chia Seed Chocolate Pudding ..................................................................................... 71
12. Low-Carb Pumpkin Pie Bites ....................................................................................... 71
13. Chocolate-Covered Almonds ....................................................................................... 72
14. Keto Peanut Butter Cups .............................................................................................. 72
15. Lemon Protein Bars ....................................................................................................... 73
16. Chocolate-Dipped Strawberries .................................................................................. 74
17. No-Bake Protein Cheesecake Bites ............................................................................ 74
18. Keto Chocolate Pudding ............................................................................................... 75
19. Low-Carb Raspberry Sorbet ........................................................................................ 75
20. Keto Lemon Bars ........................................................................................................... 76
21. Keto Chocolate Chip Cookies ...................................................................................... 77
22. Keto Strawberry Cheesecake ...................................................................................... 77

## CHAPTER 7: DRINKS ....................................................................................................... 79

1. Protein Smoothie with Almond Butter ........................................................................... 79
2. Green Protein Smoothie ................................................................................................. 79
3. Almond Milk Protein Shake ............................................................................................ 80
4. Collagen-Infused Lemonade .......................................................................................... 80
5. Chocolate Almond Protein Shake .................................................................................. 81
6. Coconut Water Protein Drink ......................................................................................... 81
7. Matcha Protein Latte ....................................................................................................... 82
8. Iced Coffee Protein Shake .............................................................................................. 82
9. Green Tea with Ginger and Lemon ............................................................................... 83
10. Low-Carb Chocolate Milkshake ................................................................................... 83
11. Coconut Protein Smoothie ............................................................................................ 84
12. Protein-Packed Mocha Shake ...................................................................................... 84
13. Cucumber Mint Protein Smoothie ............................................................................... 85
14. Protein-Rich Fruit Smoothie ......................................................................................... 86
15. Iced Matcha Protein Latte ............................................................................................ 86
16. Protein-Packed Coconut Smoothie ............................................................................. 87
17. Mocha Protein Latte ...................................................................................................... 87
18. Protein-Packed Green Juice ........................................................................................ 88
19. Strawberry Protein Smoothie ....................................................................................... 88
20. Tropical Protein Shake .................................................................................................. 89

## CHAPTER 8: MEAL PLANNING & TIPS ......................................................................... 90

- Sample Weekly Meal Plan for Beginners ............................................................................................................. 90
- Meal Prep Tips and Tricks for Time Efficiency .................................................................................................... 91
- How to Track Your Macros and Progress .......................................................................................................... 92
- How to Measure Portion Sizes ........................................................................................................................... 92
- Staying on Track with Your Goals ...................................................................................................................... 93
- Practical Tips for Sticking to the Diet .................................................................................................................. 93
- The Importance of Hydration .............................................................................................................................. 93
- Tips on Staying Hydrated and Supporting Fat Loss ............................................................................................ 93

# APPENDIX ................................................................................................................................................ 95
- Frequently Asked Questions (FAQ) .................................................................................................................... 95
- Glossary of Key Terms ....................................................................................................................................... 95
- Conversion Table for UK & US Measurements .................................................................................................. 96
- Resources & Recommended Tools .................................................................................................................... 96

# Welcome to Your High-Protein, Low-Carb Journey

Welcome to your High-Protein, Low-Carb Journey—transformative ways of eating that will not only help you achieves your fitness goals but also improve your overall health and wellbeing. This diet is more than just a way to lose weight; it is a lifestyle change that will support muscle growth, enhance energy levels, and keep you feeling fuller for longer.

Whether you're looking to lose weight, build lean muscle, or simply enjoy a healthier way of eating, this High-Protein, Low-Carb Diet offers numerous benefits. It's about nourishing your body with wholesome, nutrient-dense foods while cutting back on sugars and processed carbohydrates.

In this book, you'll find easy-to-follow, delicious recipes designed to support this lifestyle, with meals that are simple to prepare and full of flavour. Together, we'll explore why this approach works, how it functions, and how to implement it in your everyday routine for lasting results.

## What is the High-Protein, Low-Carb Diet?

The High-Protein, Low-Carb Diet is a dietary strategy that focuses on increasing protein intake while significantly reducing the consumption of carbohydrates.

Protein: Protein is a vital macronutrient responsible for building and repairing tissues, making enzymes and hormones, and supporting muscle growth. It is the key player in creating a lean, strong physique, making it essential for both weight loss and muscle building.

Carbohydrates: Carbs are usually the body's preferred source of energy, but when consumed in excess, they can lead to fat storage and blood sugar spikes. In a low-carb diet, carbs are reduced to shift the body's fuel source from glucose (carbs) to stored fat.

This diet encourages you to eat protein-rich foods such as lean meats, fish, eggs, and plant-based sources like tofu and legumes, while avoiding high-carb foods such as bread, pasta, and sugary snacks. The idea is that by reducing carbs, your body burns fat for energy, promoting fat loss and enhancing muscle gain.

In short, the High-Protein, Low-Carb Diet is about balancing your macronutrients in a way that encourages your body to burn fat more efficiently, build lean muscle, and maintain stable blood sugar levels throughout the day.

## Why Choose a High-Protein, Low-Carb Diet?

There are numerous reasons why people opt for a high-protein, low-carb diet, from weight loss to improved performance in physical activity. Here's why you should consider it:

**Effective for Weight Loss:**
This diet helps reduce your overall calorie intake by keeping you full for longer periods, reducing the likelihood of snacking between meals. Lowering your carb intake also forces your body to burn fat for fuel, leading to fat loss.

**Supports Muscle Growth:**
Protein is the foundation of muscle tissue, and consuming more protein while exercising helps your body repair and build muscle. This is particularly important if you're looking to increase lean muscle mass or recover from intense workouts.

**Improves Energy and Mental Clarity:**
By stabilising blood sugar levels, a high-protein, low-carb diet can help avoid the energy crashes associated with high-carb meals. You'll find yourself feeling more alert and focused throughout the day, with sustained energy.

**Better Blood Sugar Control:**
For individuals with insulin resistance or those at risk of diabetes, a low-carb diet can significantly improve insulin sensitivity and help regulate blood sugar levels.

**Sustained Satiety:**
Protein helps control hunger by promoting feelings of fullness. This diet reduces the likelihood of overeating, making it easier to stick to your nutritional goals.

## How Does This Diet Work?

When you follow a High-Protein, Low-Carb Diet, your body begins to use fat as its primary energy source instead of carbohydrates. Here's how it works:

**Reduced Carbohydrate Intake:**
Carbs are broken down into glucose (sugar), which is used for energy. When you reduce carbs, the body turns to fat stores for energy. This process is known as fat oxidation.

**Ketosis (When Carbs Are Drastically Reduced):**
If you reduce your carbs to a very low level, your liver starts converting fat into ketones, an alternative fuel source. This metabolic state is known as ketosis and is the basis of the ketogenic diet. It helps the body burn fat more efficiently while preserving lean muscle mass.

**Increased Protein Intake:**
Protein helps in muscle repair and growth. When you consume protein-rich foods, your body uses it to rebuild and repair muscles after exercise. Additionally, protein keeps you feeling full longer, which helps prevent unnecessary snacking and overeating.

**Stable Blood Sugar Levels:**
By reducing carbohydrate intake, the body doesn't experience the spikes and crashes in blood sugar that often result from eating high-carb foods. This leads to more stable energy throughout the day, preventing fatigue and irritability.

In essence, this diet encourages your body to become more efficient at using fat for fuel while supporting muscle growth and repair through increased protein intake.

## The Science behind Protein and Carbs

The relationship between protein and carbohydrates is fundamental to how the High-Protein, Low-Carb Diet functions:

Protein is an essential nutrient that plays a role in nearly every function within the body. By increasing protein intake, your body can repair and grow muscle, regulate hormone levels, and enhance overall metabolism. Protein also has a higher thermic effect than carbohydrates and fats, meaning the body burns more calories during the digestion of protein.

Carbohydrates, on the other hand, are typically the body's first choice for energy. However, excess carbs—especially refined carbs—are stored as fat, which can lead to weight gain. By cutting down on carbs, your body will turn to fat stores for energy, promoting weight loss and fat burning. This switch from carbs to fat as the primary energy source is what makes the high-protein, low-carb diet so effective for fat loss.

## Key Benefits of the High-Protein, Low-Carb Approach

Fat Loss: By cutting carbs and increasing protein, your body is forced to burn stored fat for energy, resulting in fat loss while maintaining lean muscle.

**Muscle Preservation and Growth**: Protein is crucial for building and repairing muscles, making it an excellent diet choice for those who want to preserve muscle mass during weight loss or actively build muscle.

**Improved Metabolism:** The high thermic effect of protein increases your metabolism, which means you burn more calories even while resting.

**Better Appetite Control**: Protein helps to regulate hunger hormones, keeping you feeling full longer and making it easier to control portion sizes.

**Enhanced Mental Focus:** Stable blood sugar levels lead to clearer thinking and improved cognitive performance, helping you stay sharp throughout the day.

**Improved Insulin Sensitivity**: A low-carb diet can help regulate blood sugar levels and improve insulin sensitivity, which is beneficial for overall health, particularly for those with or at risk for type 2 diabetes.

## How to Use This Cookbook

This cookbook is designed to be both practical and accessible, whether you're a beginner or already familiar with the high-protein, low-carb lifestyle. Here's how to get the most out of it:

**Start with the Basics**: Begin by understanding the key principles of the diet, the benefits, and how your body will respond. The first chapter provides a solid foundation.

**Follow the Recipes:** Each recipe has been crafted to be simple, delicious, and easy to prepare. The recipes in this book are designed to fit seamlessly into your daily routine while adhering to the high-protein, low-carb guidelines.

**Plan Your Meals:** Use the meal planning tips and recipes in this book to create balanced, healthy meals for the week. Meal planning will save you time and ensure you stay on track with your goals.

**Track you're Progress**: Keep track of how you feel and any changes in your body. This will help you stay motivated and see the progress you're making.

## How to Get Started

**Set Clear Goals:** Decide on what you hope to achieve with this diet—whether it's weight loss, muscle gain, or better overall health. Setting specific goals will keep you motivated.

**Start Slow**: If you're new to the high-protein, low-carb lifestyle, begin by gradually reducing carbs and increasing protein. Don't feel like you need to make drastic changes overnight.

**Focus on Quality**: Choose high-quality protein sources and nutrient-dense, low-carb vegetables to maximise the benefits of the diet.

**Stay Consistent:** Consistency is key to success. Stick to the meal plan, keep an eye on your macros, and be patient as your body adjusts.

With this solid foundation, you're now ready to begin your high-protein, low-carb journey. Let's dive into the recipes that will guide you every step of the way, ensuring that you reach your health and fitness goals, one delicious meal at a time.

# Chapter 1:

# High-Protein, Low-Carb Diet Basics

## The Essentials of a High-Protein, Low-Carb Diet

The High-Protein, Low-Carb Diet is a powerful approach to eating that focuses on boosting protein intake while reducing carbohydrates. This dietary strategy is designed to promote fat loss, muscle preservation, and improved metabolic health by shifting the body's primary energy source from carbohydrates to fat.

At its core, this diet involves choosing high-quality protein sources, such as meat, fish, eggs, and plant-based alternatives, while avoiding refined carbohydrates and foods that spike blood sugar levels. By significantly reducing carbs, particularly from processed sources, the body shifts its energy metabolism, encouraging fat burning and muscle development.

The high-protein component ensures your body has the necessary building blocks for muscle repair and growth, while the low-carb aspect helps to stabilise insulin levels, prevent fat storage, and reduce hunger. This balance of nutrients supports long-term weight management and improved fitness outcomes.

## Understanding Macronutrients

The key to a successful high-protein, low-carb diet lies in understanding the three primary macronutrients that make up the foods you eat: proteins, fats, and carbohydrates. Each macronutrient plays a different role in your body and has its unique benefits. Let's break them down:

Protein: Protein is made up of amino acids, which are essential for building and repairing body tissues. It is a key component in the growth of muscles, organs, skin, and hormones. It also plays a crucial role in the immune system and enzyme production.

Fat: Fat is a crucial energy source and helps in the absorption of fat-soluble vitamins (A, D, E, and K). Healthy fats, such as those found in avocados, olive oil, and nuts, are vital for brain function, hormone regulation, and joint health.

Carbohydrates: Carbs are the body's main energy source, providing fuel for daily activities. However, not all carbs are created equal. Simple carbs, like those found in sugary snacks and processed foods, can cause blood sugar spikes and contribute to fat storage. Complex carbs, found in whole grains and vegetables, provide more sustained energy and are richer in fibre.

On a High-Protein, Low-Carb Diet, the focus is on increasing the proportion of protein and healthy fats while significantly reducing carbohydrates, especially refined ones. This helps the body shift into a fat-burning state while maintaining muscle mass.

## What Are Proteins, Fats, and Carbs?

Proteins: Proteins are made of amino acids, which are the building blocks of the body. There are nine essential amino acids that the body cannot make, so they must come from food sources. Protein plays a vital role in repairing tissues, building muscles, supporting metabolic processes, and keeping your immune system strong.

- Common sources of protein include:
- Meat (beef, chicken, pork, etc.)
- Fish and seafood

- Eggs
- Legumes and beans (for plant-based options)
- Dairy products like Greek yogurt and cottage cheese
- Tofu and tempeh (for vegetarians/vegans)

Fats: Fats are a concentrated source of energy that the body uses for various essential functions. They help absorb nutrients, maintain cell structure, and regulate body temperature. Not all fats are the same, and healthy fats (such as those found in avocados, nuts, seeds, and olive oil) are essential for heart health, brain function, and hormone production.

**Key fat sources include:**

- Avocados
- Nuts and seeds
- Olive oil and coconut oil
- Fatty fish (like salmon, mackerel, and sardines)

Carbohydrates: Carbohydrates are the body's primary source of fuel, especially for high-energy activities like exercise. Carbs are broken down into glucose (sugar), which the body uses for energy. However, refined carbs (like white bread, pasta, and sugary snacks) can cause spikes in blood sugar, leading to fat storage.

- Healthy, complex carbs include:
- Leafy greens (spinach, kale, etc.)
- Cruciferous vegetables (broccoli, cauliflower)
- Berries and other low-carb fruits
- Sweet potatoes and squash (in moderation)

## The Role of Each Macronutrient in Your Body

Each of the three macronutrients plays a distinct and critical role:

Protein: Supports muscle repair and growth, helps regulate hormones, and strengthens the immune system. It also increases the thermic effect of food (TEF), which means your body burns more calories digesting protein than other macronutrients.

Fat: Provides long-lasting energy, helps absorb vitamins, and contributes to the production of hormones. Fats are essential for brain health and maintaining cellular integrity.

Carbohydrates: Serve as a fast source of energy. Complex carbs are essential for providing fibre, which supports digestion and overall health.

On a high-protein, low-carb diet, protein and healthy fats take centre stage, supporting muscle growth, fat-burning, and energy regulation, while carbohydrates are reduced to a level that encourages the body to shift from burning glucose to burning fat.

## How the High-Protein, Low-Carb Diet Works

When you reduce your carbohydrate intake, your body enters a metabolic state known as fat-burning. Since carbs are typically the body's main fuel source, lowering carbs forces the body to rely on stored fat for energy. This process not only helps with fat loss but also provides consistent energy levels throughout the day.

By consuming more protein, the body has enough fuel for muscle repair and growth. Additionally, protein helps keep hunger at bay by increasing feelings of fullness and satiety.

For those who dramatically reduce carbs, the body may enter a state of ketosis, where fat is converted into ketones for energy. Ketosis is the hallmark of the ketogenic diet, but even without reaching full ketosis, the low-carb approach still encourages fat burning, muscle preservation, and improved metabolic health.

## The Process of Ketosis and Fat-Burning

Ketosis is a natural metabolic state that occurs when the body has limited access to carbohydrates. In this state, the liver begins to produce ketones from fat, which can be used as an alternative energy source for the brain and muscles. By following a low-carb diet, you effectively push your body into fat-burning mode, encouraging the use of fat for energy instead of carbohydrates.

While ketosis is more common in extremely low-carb diets like the ketogenic diet, even a moderate reduction in carbs can increase fat oxidation (the burning of fat for energy) and promote sustained weight loss over time.

## Why Protein is Important

Protein is the foundation of your body's structure, serving as the building block for muscles, bones, skin, and tissues. Here's why it's so crucial:

Building Muscle: Protein is essential for muscle repair and growth. After exercise, the body needs sufficient protein to recover and rebuild muscle tissue. For anyone looking to increase muscle mass or improve strength, protein is the key nutrient.

Repairing Tissues: Protein helps repair damaged tissues, from minor injuries to larger wounds, ensuring proper recovery.

Boosting Metabolism: Protein has a higher thermic effect than fats and carbohydrates. This means that your body burns more calories digesting and metabolising protein than it does for the other macronutrients.

## How Carbs Affect Your Body

Carbohydrates, particularly refined ones, can have a significant impact on your blood sugar levels. When you consume high-carb foods, the body breaks them down into glucose, which enters the bloodstream and raises blood sugar levels. If you consume more carbs than your body needs, the excess glucose is converted to fat and stored.

While carbs are an essential energy source, reducing the intake of refined carbs (such as sugary snacks, white bread, and pasta) can help prevent fat storage, support stable energy levels, and reduce hunger throughout the day.

## The Truth Behind Low-Carb Eating

The low-carb approach is not about completely eliminating carbs from your diet. Rather, it focuses on reducing refined carbs and replacing them with nutrient-dense, whole foods that are naturally low in carbohydrates, such as vegetables, healthy fats, and protein-rich foods.

This approach encourages the body to burn fat for fuel, instead of relying on glucose from carbohydrates. By focusing on whole foods and healthy fats, a low-carb diet can enhance weight loss, increase energy levels, and improve overall health.

**Top Benefits of Following a High-Protein, Low-Carb Diet**
**Weight Loss:**
A high-protein, low-carb diet helps the body burn fat for fuel, leading to effective weight loss while maintaining lean muscle mass.

Muscle Gain:
Protein is essential for muscle growth. A diet high in protein supports muscle recovery and promotes muscle-building, particularly when combined with strength training.

Increased Energy Levels:
By stabilising blood sugar levels, this diet prevents energy crashes and provides sustained energy throughout the day.

**Reduced Hunger:**
Protein promotes feelings of fullness and satiety, which can reduce overall calorie intake and prevent overeating.

## Foods to Embrace and Foods to Avoid

List of Protein-Rich Foods and Low-Carb Vegetables
Protein-rich foods: Chicken, turkey, lean beef, eggs, fish (salmon, mackerel), tofu, tempeh, Greek yogurt, cottage cheese, legumes (beans, lentils).

Low-carb vegetables: Spinach, kale, broccoli, cauliflower, zucchini, bell peppers, cucumber, mushrooms, asparagus, green beans.

## Foods to Cut Back On or Eliminate

Refined carbs: White bread, pasta, cakes, pastries, sugary snacks.

Sugary beverages: Soft drinks, sweetened juices, and sugary coffee drinks.

Processed foods: Fast food, packaged snacks, and pre-packaged meals.

This detailed chapter sets the stage for your high-protein, low-carb journey by explaining the science, benefits, and practical steps behind the diet. Let me know if you'd like more chapters or additional information on any section!

# Chapter 2:

# Breakfast Recipes

## Overview of a High-Protein Breakfast

High-protein breakfast is essential for kickstarting your day with the right kind of energy. Protein is a macronutrient that supports muscle repair, growth, and satiety—helping to keep you full until your next meal. In addition to providing energy, a high-protein breakfast stabilises blood sugar levels, reducing cravings for sugary snacks or carb-heavy foods that can cause energy crashes later in the day.

On a high-protein, low-carb diet, breakfast plays a crucial role in setting the tone for the day. By incorporating lean proteins and healthy fats, you can enjoy meals that keep you full and focused, all while staying on track with your health and fitness goals. This chapter features a variety of delicious, simple recipes that are packed with protein and low in carbs, ensuring you stay satisfied and fuelled throughout your busy mornings.

These recipes are designed to be easily adaptable, quick to prepare, and perfect for anyone following a high-protein, low-carb lifestyle. Let's dive in!

## 1. Spinach and Mushroom Scrambled Eggs

Prep Time: 5 minutes
Cook Time: 10 minutes
Servings: 1

Ingredients:

2 large eggs

1/2 cup fresh spinach (or frozen, thawed)

1/4 cup mushrooms, sliced

Salt and pepper to taste

1 tbsp olive oil or butter

Instructions:

Heat a pan over medium heat and add olive oil or butter.

Add the mushrooms and sauté for 3-4 minutes until softened.

Toss in the spinach and cook for 1-2 minutes until wilted.

Crack the eggs into the pan and scramble them with the veggies until fully cooked.

Season with salt and pepper to taste, and serve warm.

Why it's great:
This breakfast is rich in protein and fibre, providing the perfect balance of nutrients to start your day. The mushrooms and spinach are packed with antioxidants and fibre, supporting overall health.

## 2. Greek Yogurt with Mixed Berries and Almonds

Prep Time: 5 minutes
Cook Time: 0 minutes
Servings: 1

Ingredients:

1 cup plain Greek yogurt (unsweetened)

1/4 cup mixed berries (blueberries, raspberries, strawberries)

1 tbsp sliced almonds

1 tsp honey (optional)

Instructions:

Spoon the Greek yogurt into a bowl.

Top with mixed berries and sliced almonds.

Drizzle with honey if desired.

Stir and enjoy!

Why it's great:
Greek yogurt is a great source of protein and probiotics, while the berries provide antioxidants, and almonds add a satisfying crunch. This is an easy, nutrient-dense breakfast that supports gut health and keeps you full for longer.

## 3. Chia Seed Pudding with Coconut Milk

Prep Time: 5 minutes
Cook Time: 0 minutes (requires overnight refrigeration)
Servings: 1

Ingredients:

3 tbsp chia seeds

1 cup unsweetened coconut milk (or almond milk)

1 tsp vanilla extract

1/2 tbsp sweetener of choice (stevia, honey, or maple syrup)

Fresh berries for topping (optional)

Instructions:

In a jar or bowl, combine the chia seeds, coconut milk, vanilla extract, and sweetener.

Stir well and cover the bowl. Refrigerate overnight or for at least 4 hours.

In the morning, stir the pudding and top with fresh berries if desired.

Why it's great:
Chia seeds are an excellent source of protein, fibre, and omega-3 fatty acids, making this a satisfying breakfast that will keep you feeling full. The coconut milk adds a creamy texture, and it's a perfect make-ahead meal for busy mornings.

## 4. Egg Muffins with Bacon and Spinach

Prep Time: 10 minutes
Cook Time: 15 minutes
Servings: 6 muffins

Ingredients:

6 large eggs

1/4 cup spinach, chopped

4 strips of bacon, cooked and crumbled

1/4 cup shredded cheddar cheese (optional)

Salt and pepper to taste

1 tbsp olive oil (for greasing muffin tin)

Instructions:

Preheat your oven to 190°C (375°F). Grease a muffin tin with olive oil.

In a large bowl, whisk together the eggs, chopped spinach, crumbled bacon, cheddar cheese, salt, and pepper.

Pour the egg mixture into the muffin tin, filling each cup about 3/4 full.

Bake for 15-20 minutes until the eggs are fully set.

Allow the muffins to cool slightly before serving.

Why it's great:
These egg muffins are a perfect on-the-go breakfast or snack. Packed with protein from the eggs and bacon, they are easy to make ahead and provide a high-protein, low-carb option for your mornings.

## 5. Protein Pancakes with Sugar-Free Syrup

Prep Time: 5 minutes
Cook Time: 10 minutes
Servings: 2 pancakes

Ingredients:

1 scoop vanilla protein powder

2 large eggs

1/4 cup unsweetened almond milk (or milk of choice)

1/2 tsp baking powder

1/4 tsp cinnamon

Sugar-free syrup for topping (optional)

Instructions:

In a bowl, whisk together the protein powder, eggs, almond milk, baking powder, and cinnamon until smooth.

Heat a non-stick pan over medium heat and lightly grease it.

Pour small amounts of batter onto the pan to form pancakes. Cook for 2-3 minutes on each side or until golden brown.

Serve with sugar-free syrup if desired.

Why it's great:
These protein pancakes provide a high dose of protein with minimal carbs. Perfect for a post-workout breakfast or a filling meal to start your day.

## 6. Avocado and Egg Breakfast Bowl

Prep Time: 5 minutes
Cook Time: 5 minutes
Servings: 1

Ingredients:

1 ripe avocado

2 large eggs

Salt and pepper to taste

A handful of cherry tomatoes (optional)

1 tbsp olive oil (optional)

Instructions:

Slice the avocado and scoop out the flesh, placing it in a bowl.

In a non-stick pan, heat the olive oil (if using) and fry the eggs to your liking (sunny side up, scrambled, etc.).

Top the avocado with the fried eggs and season with salt and pepper.

Add cherry tomatoes for extra freshness and flavour, if desired.

Why it's great:
Avocados are rich in healthy fats and fibre, making them an excellent choice for breakfast. Paired with eggs, this bowl provides a perfect combination of protein and healthy fats to fuel your morning.

## 7. Cottage Cheese and Cucumber Salad

Prep Time: 5 minutes
Cook Time: 0 minutes
Servings: 1

Ingredients:

1 cup cottage cheese (low-fat or full-fat)

1/2 cucumber, sliced

Salt and pepper to taste

1 tbsp fresh dill (optional)

Instructions:

In a bowl, combine the cottage cheese and sliced cucumber.

Season with salt and pepper and stir gently.

Garnish with fresh dill for extra flavour and enjoy!

Why it's great:
This refreshing salad is packed with protein and calcium from cottage cheese, while the cucumber adds a satisfying crunch and hydration. It's a light but filling breakfast option, perfect for a quick start to your day.

## 8. Almond Flour Banana Bread (Sugar-Free)

Prep Time: 10 minutes
Cook Time: 40-45 minutes
Servings: 8 slices

Ingredients:

2 ripe bananas, mashed

1 1/2 cups almond flour

2 large eggs

1/4 cup unsweetened almond milk

1 tsp vanilla extract

1/2 tsp baking soda

1/2 tsp cinnamon

1/4 cup walnuts (optional)

Instructions:

Preheat the oven to 175°C (350°F). Grease a loaf pan.

In a bowl, mix together mashed bananas, eggs, almond milk, and vanilla extract.

Add almond flour, baking soda, cinnamon, and stir until combined.

Pour the batter into the loaf pan and sprinkle walnuts on top.

Bake for 40-45 minutes or until a toothpick inserted comes out clean.

Let cool before slicing.

Why it's great:
This banana bread is a sugar-free, low-carb alternative to traditional banana bread, made with almond flour for extra protein and healthy fats. It's a perfect treat for breakfast or a snack.

## 9. Zucchini and Feta Omelet

Prep Time: 5 minutes
Cook Time: 10 minutes
Servings: 1

Ingredients:

2 large eggs

1/4 cup zucchini, grated

1/4 cup feta cheese, crumbled

Salt and pepper to taste

1 tbsp olive oil or butter

Instructions:

Heat olive oil or butter in a non-stick frying pan over medium heat.

Add the grated zucchini to the pan and sauté for 2-3 minutes until soft.

Whisk the eggs in a bowl, then pour them over the zucchini in the pan.

Sprinkle the crumbled feta cheese on top of the eggs.

Cook the omelet for 3-4 minutes until the eggs are set, then flip it to cook the other side for an additional 2 minutes.

Season with salt and pepper to taste and serve immediately.

Why it's great:
This omelet is a delicious and filling breakfast, rich in protein from eggs and feta. Zucchini adds a light, refreshing crunch while keeping the carbs low. The combination of protein and healthy fats will keep you satisfied throughout the morning.

## 10. Cinnamon Flaxseed Porridge

Prep Time: 5 minutes
Cook Time: 10 minutes
Servings: 1

Ingredients:

2 tbsp ground flaxseeds

1 cup unsweetened almond milk (or any milk of choice)

1/2 tsp ground cinnamon

1 tbsp chia seeds

Stevia or sweetener of choice (optional)

Instructions:

In a small saucepan, combine the flaxseeds, almond milk, cinnamon, and chia seeds.

Heat over medium heat, stirring occasionally, until the mixture thickens, about 5-7 minutes.

Once the porridge reaches your desired consistency, remove from heat.

Stir in your sweetener (if using) and serve hot.

Why it's great:
Flaxseeds are an excellent source of plant-based protein and omega-3 fatty acids, while chia seeds provide additional fibre and protein. This porridge is a warm, filling breakfast that will keep your blood sugar stable and hunger at bay.

## 11. Peanut Butter Chia Smoothie

Prep Time: 5 minutes
Cook Time: 0 minutes
Servings: 1

Ingredients:

1 tbsp natural peanut butter

1 tbsp chia seeds

1/2 cup unsweetened almond milk

1/2 cup Greek yogurt (unsweetened)

1/4 cup ice cubes

1/2 tsp vanilla extract

Stevia or sweetener of choice (optional)

Instructions:

Add the peanut butter, chia seeds, almond milk, Greek yogurt, ice cubes, and vanilla extract to a blender.

Blend on high for 30-40 seconds until smooth and creamy.

Taste and add stevia or your preferred sweetener, if desired.

Pour into a glass and enjoy immediately.

Why it's great:
This smoothie is packed with protein from the peanut butter and Greek yogurt, and the chia seeds add a dose of fibre and omega-3s. It's a perfect quick breakfast for busy mornings or as a post-workout meal.

## 12. Low-Carb Protein Oats

Prep Time: 5 minutes
Cook Time: 10 minutes
Servings: 1

Ingredients:

2 tbsp oat bran

1 scoop vanilla protein powder

1 cup unsweetened almond milk

1 tbsp ground flaxseeds

1/4 tsp cinnamon

1 tbsp almond butter (optional)

Instructions:

In a saucepan, bring the almond milk to a gentle simmer.

Stir in the oat bran, protein powder, cinnamon, and flaxseeds.

Cook for 5-7 minutes, stirring occasionally, until the mixture thickens to a porridge-like consistency.

Top with almond butter for added richness (optional), and serve warm.

Why it's great:
This low-carb, protein-packed porridge provides the benefits of oats without the high carb load. Oat bran is lower in carbs than regular oats, and the protein powder helps ensure that you get a substantial amount of protein to start your day.

## 13. Cottage Cheese and Chive Breakfast Bowl

Prep Time: 5 minutes
Cook Time: 0 minutes
Servings: 1

Ingredients:

1 cup cottage cheese (low-fat or full-fat)

1/4 cup chopped chives

Salt and pepper to taste

1/4 cup cucumber, diced

1 tbsp olive oil (optional)

Instructions:

In a bowl, combine the cottage cheese, chopped chives, and diced cucumber.

Drizzle with olive oil if desired, and season with salt and pepper to taste.

Stir well and enjoy immediately.

Why it's great:
Cottage cheese is a rich source of protein, while cucumber adds a refreshing crunch and a good dose of hydration. Chives bring an aromatic flavour, making this a delicious, quick breakfast.

## 14. Smoked Salmon and Avocado Breakfast Bowl

Prep Time: 5 minutes
Cook Time: 0 minutes
Servings: 1

Ingredients:

2 oz smoked salmon

1/2 avocado, sliced

1 tbsp lemon juice

Salt and pepper to taste

A handful of mixed greens (optional)

Instructions:

In a bowl, place the smoked salmon and sliced avocado.

Drizzle with lemon juice and season with salt and pepper.

Add a handful of mixed greens for extra nutrients (optional), and serve immediately.

Why it's great:
Smoked salmon provides a healthy dose of omega-3 fatty acids, while avocado adds healthy fats and fibre. This breakfast is quick, refreshing, and nutrient-packed, making it perfect for busy mornings.

## 15. Protein-Packed Smoothie Bowl

Prep Time: 5 minutes
Cook Time: 0 minutes
Servings: 1

Ingredients:

1 scoop protein powder

1/2 cup frozen berries

1/4 cup unsweetened almond milk

1 tbsp almond butter

1 tbsp chia seeds

Instructions:

In a blender, combine the protein powder, frozen berries, almond milk, almond butter, and chia seeds.

Blend until smooth, adding more almond milk if necessary for desired consistency.

Pour into a bowl and top with additional chia seeds, nuts, or berries, if desired.

Why it's great:
This smoothie bowl is packed with protein, healthy fats, and fibre, making it a perfect breakfast for muscle recovery and energy. It's a fun and visually appealing way to enjoy your morning nutrients.

## 16. Avocado, Bacon, and Egg Breakfast Cups

Prep Time: 5 minutes
Cook Time: 10 minutes
Servings: 2

Ingredients:

2 ripe avocados

2 large eggs

2 strips of bacon, cooked and crumbled

Salt and pepper to taste

A pinch of paprika (optional)

Instructions:

Preheat the oven to 190°C (375°F).

Cut the avocados in half and remove the pit. Use a spoon to scoop out a little bit of the flesh to make room for the egg.

Place the avocado halves in a baking dish, and crack an egg into each half.

Sprinkle with salt, pepper, and a pinch of paprika.

Bake for 10-12 minutes, or until the eggs are cooked to your desired consistency.

Top with crumbled bacon and serve immediately.

**Why it's great:**
This breakfast bowl combines the richness of avocado with the savoury crunch of bacon and protein from the egg. It's a filling, satisfying breakfast that is low in carbs and high in healthy fats, making it perfect for a low-carb lifestyle.

## 17. Low-Carb Egg and Veggie Scramble

Prep Time: 5 minutes
Cook Time: 10 minutes
Servings: 1

Ingredients:

2 large eggs

1/4 cup bell pepper, chopped

1/4 cup onion, chopped

1/4 cup spinach, chopped

1 tbsp olive oil or butter

Salt and pepper to taste

Instructions:

Heat olive oil or butter in a pan over medium heat.

Add the bell pepper and onion to the pan, and sauté until softened, about 3-4 minutes.

Add the spinach and cook until wilted, about 2 minutes.

Crack the eggs into the pan and scramble with the vegetables until fully cooked.

Season with salt and pepper to taste, and serve immediately.

**Why it's great:**
This veggie-packed scramble is a great way to start your day with plenty of protein and healthy vegetables. The combination of spinach, bell pepper, and onion provides antioxidants, while the eggs give you a solid protein boost to keep you full.

## 18. Almond Flour Pancakes with Greek Yogurt

Prep Time: 5 minutes
Cook Time: 10 minutes
Servings: 2 pancakes

Ingredients:

1/2 cup almond flour

1 large egg

1/4 cup unsweetened almond milk

1/2 tsp vanilla extract

1/2 tsp baking powder

A pinch of salt

Greek yogurt (unsweetened) for topping

Fresh berries for garnish (optional)

Instructions:

In a bowl, whisk together the almond flour, egg, almond milk, vanilla extract, baking powder, and a pinch of salt until smooth.

Heat a non-stick pan over medium heat and lightly grease it with butter or oil.

Pour small amounts of the batter into the pan, forming pancakes. Cook for 2-3 minutes on each side or until golden brown.

Serve with a dollop of Greek yogurt and top with fresh berries, if desired.

Why it's great:
These almond flour pancakes are a perfect alternative to traditional pancakes, offering a higher protein and lower carb content. Topped with Greek yogurt, they become an even more protein-packed breakfast that will leave you feeling satisfied without the sugar crash.

## 19. Tofu Scramble with Veggies

Prep Time: 5 minutes
Cook Time: 10 minutes
Servings: 1

Ingredients:

1/2 block firm tofu, crumbled

1/4 cup bell peppers, chopped

1/4 cup mushrooms, chopped

1/4 cup spinach, chopped

1 tbsp olive oil

1/4 tsp turmeric (optional)

Salt and pepper to taste

Instructions:

Heat olive oil in a pan over medium heat.

Add the bell peppers, mushrooms, and spinach to the pan and sauté for 3-4 minutes.

Add the crumbled tofu to the pan and cook for another 3-4 minutes, stirring occasionally.

Add turmeric, salt, and pepper, and mix well.

Cook for an additional 2 minutes, then serve.

Why it's great:
This tofu scramble is a vegan-friendly alternative to scrambled eggs, packed with protein and veggies. Tofu is an excellent source of plant-based protein, and the addition of spinach and bell peppers ensures you get plenty of fibre and vitamins to start your day.

## 20. Protein-Packed Smoothie

Prep Time: 5 minutes
Cook Time: 0 minutes

Servings: 1

Ingredients:

1 scoop protein powder (vanilla or chocolate)

1/2 banana

1/2 cup unsweetened almond milk

1 tbsp almond butter

1/2 cup spinach

A handful of ice cubes

Instructions:

In a blender, combine the protein powder, banana, almond milk, almond butter, spinach, and ice cubes.

Blend on high for 30-40 seconds until smooth and creamy.

Pour into a glass and enjoy immediately.

Why it's great:
This smoothie is packed with protein from the powder and almond butter, plus a good dose of greens from the spinach. It's a quick, easy, and delicious way to fuel your morning with minimal effort.

# Chapter 3: Lunch Recipes

## Overview of a High-Protein Lunch

Lunch is an important opportunity to refuel your body with the essential nutrients needed to sustain you through the afternoon. A high-protein, low-carb lunch is not only key for supporting muscle growth and fat loss, but it also helps maintain steady energy levels, curbing hunger and preventing mid-afternoon slumps. Protein-rich foods aid in muscle repair, enhance metabolism, and promote feelings of fullness, ensuring you don't reach for unhealthy snacks before dinner.

On a high-protein, low-carb diet, lunch should ideally include lean proteins, healthy fats, and low-carb vegetables. With the right balance of these macronutrients, you'll stay satisfied, fuel your body for the rest of the day, and keep your metabolism working efficiently.

In this chapter, you'll find 20 satisfying, nutrient-dense lunch recipes that align with your high-protein, low-carb goals. Whether you're looking for a refreshing salad, a savoury bowl, or a filling wrap, there's something here to suit every taste.

## 1. Grilled Chicken and Avocado Salad

Prep Time: 10 minutes
Cook Time: 15 minutes
Servings: 1

Ingredients:

1 chicken breast, grilled and sliced

1/2 avocado, diced

1 cup mixed salad greens (spinach, arugula, etc.)

1/4 cup cherry tomatoes, halved

1 tbsp olive oil

1 tbsp lemon juice

Salt and pepper to taste

Instructions:

Grill the chicken breast until fully cooked, about 6-7 minutes per side. Slice thinly.

In a bowl, combine the mixed salad greens, cherry tomatoes, and avocado.

Drizzle with olive oil and lemon juice, and toss gently.

Top with the grilled chicken and season with salt and pepper to taste.

Serve immediately.

Why it's great:
This salad combines protein from the chicken with healthy fats from avocado, making it a filling and satisfying meal that won't leave you feeling hungry. It's a light yet nutrient-packed dish that is perfect for a midday boost.

## 2. Tuna Salad Lettuce Wraps

Prep Time: 5 minutes

Cook Time: 0 minutes
Servings: 1

Ingredients:

1 can tuna in olive oil, drained

2 tbsp mayonnaise (or Greek yogurt for a lighter option)

1 tbsp mustard

Salt and pepper to taste

4 large lettuce leaves (romaine or butter lettuce)

1 tbsp chopped pickles (optional)

Instructions:

In a bowl, combine the tuna, mayonnaise, mustard, and chopped pickles.

Season with salt and pepper to taste.

Spoon the tuna mixture onto the centre of each lettuce leaf.

Wrap the leaves around the tuna mixture and enjoy.

Why it's great:
These lettuce wraps provide a low-carb alternative to a traditional sandwich, with plenty of protein from the tuna. The mayonnaise or Greek yogurt adds creaminess, while the mustard gives it a tangy kick.

## 3. Turkey and Veggie Lettuce Cups

Prep Time: 10 minutes
Cook Time: 0 minutes
Servings: 2

Ingredients:

200g ground turkey

1/4 cup bell peppers, finely chopped

1/4 cup onions, finely chopped

1 tbsp olive oil

1 tbsp soy sauce (low-sodium)

1/4 tsp garlic powder

4-5 large lettuce leaves

Salt and pepper to taste

Instructions:

Heat olive oil in a pan over medium heat. Add the ground turkey and cook until browned, about 6-7 minutes.

Add the chopped bell peppers, onions, soy sauce, garlic powder, salt, and pepper to the turkey. Cook for an additional 2-3 minutes until the vegetables are softened.

Spoon the turkey mixture into the centre of each lettuce leaf and serve immediately.

Why it's great:
These turkey and veggie lettuce cups are a healthy, low-carb alternative to tacos or wraps. They're packed with protein and fibre, and the bell peppers and onions add a delicious crunch and flavour.

## 4. Zucchini Noodles with Grilled Chicken

Prep Time: 10 minutes
Cook Time: 10 minutes
Servings: 1

Ingredients:

1 medium zucchini, spiralised into noodles

1 chicken breast, grilled and sliced

1 tbsp olive oil

1 tbsp lemon juice

1 tbsp fresh basil, chopped

Salt and pepper to taste

Instructions:

Grill the chicken breast until fully cooked, about 6-7 minutes per side. Slice thinly.

Heat olive oil in a pan over medium heat. Add the zucchini noodles and sauté for 2-3 minutes until tender.

Drizzle the zucchini noodles with lemon juice, then top with the grilled chicken and chopped basil.

Season with salt and pepper to taste and serve immediately.

Why it's great:
Zucchini noodles (or "zoodles") are a fantastic low-carb pasta alternative. Paired with lean protein from the chicken, this dish provides a light yet satisfying meal that's full of flavour and nutrition.

## 5. Egg Salad with Avocado and Mustard Dressing

Prep Time: 10 minutes
Cook Time: 10 minutes
Servings: 1

Ingredients:

2 large eggs, boiled and chopped

1/2 avocado, diced

1 tbsp mustard

1 tbsp olive oil

1 tsp lemon juice

Salt and pepper to taste

Instructions:

Boil the eggs, peel them, and chop them into small pieces.

In a bowl, mix the chopped eggs, avocado, mustard, olive oil, and lemon juice.

Season with salt and pepper to taste, and stir until combined.

Serve immediately, or chill in the fridge for later.

Why it's great:
This creamy egg salad is packed with protein and healthy fats. The avocado adds a rich texture, while the mustard dressing provides a tangy flavour, making it a refreshing and satisfying lunch.

## 6. Spicy Grilled Salmon with a Side of Cabbage Slaw

Prep Time: 5 minutes
Cook Time: 15 minutes
Servings: 1

Ingredients:

1 salmon fillet

1 tbsp olive oil

1/2 tsp paprika

1/4 tsp cayenne pepper

1/4 tsp garlic powder

Salt and pepper to taste

1 cup cabbage, shredded

1 tbsp apple cider vinegar

1 tbsp olive oil (for slaw)

Instructions:

Preheat your grill or grill pan to medium-high heat.

Brush the salmon with olive oil and season with paprika, cayenne pepper, garlic powder, salt, and pepper.

Grill the salmon for 4-5 minutes on each side, or until fully cooked.

In a separate bowl, combine the shredded cabbage with apple cider vinegar and olive oil. Toss well to coat.

Serve the grilled salmon with the cabbage slaw on the side.

Why it's great:
Salmon is rich in healthy omega-3 fatty acids and protein, while the spicy seasoning adds a burst of flavour. The cabbage slaw is a crunchy, low-carb side that complements the richness of the fish.

## 7. Lentil and Quinoa Salad with Feta Cheese

Prep Time: 10 minutes
Cook Time: 15 minutes
Servings: 1

Ingredients:

1/2 cup cooked quinoa

1/2 cup cooked lentils

1/4 cup feta cheese, crumbled

1/4 cup cherry tomatoes, halved

1 tbsp olive oil

1 tbsp balsamic vinegar

Salt and pepper to taste

Instructions:

In a bowl, combine the cooked quinoa, cooked lentils, crumbled feta cheese, and cherry tomatoes.

Drizzle with olive oil and balsamic vinegar, then toss well to combine.

Season with salt and pepper to taste and serve.

Why it's great:
This salad combines plant-based protein from lentils and quinoa with the richness of feta cheese. It's a satisfying, fibre-packed meal that supports digestion while keeping you full and energized.

## 8. Low-Carb Turkey Meatballs with Zoodles

Prep Time: 10 minutes
Cook Time: 20 minutes
Servings: 2

Ingredients:

200g ground turkey

1/4 cup almond flour

1/4 tsp garlic powder

1/4 tsp dried oregano

Salt and pepper to taste

1 tbsp olive oil

1 medium zucchini, spiralised into noodles

1/4 cup marinara sauce (low-carb)

Instructions:

Preheat the oven to 190°C (375°F).

In a bowl, mix the ground turkey, almond flour, garlic powder, oregano, salt, and pepper.

Roll the mixture into meatballs and place them on a baking tray. Bake for 15-20 minutes, or until cooked through.

Heat olive oil in a pan over medium heat, add the zucchini noodles, and sauté for 2-3 minutes until tender.

Top the zoodles with the baked turkey meatballs and marinara sauce.

Why it's great:
These turkey meatballs are a delicious, high-protein alternative to traditional meatballs. Paired with zucchini noodles, this meal is low in carbs and perfect for anyone seeking a healthy, filling lunch.

## 9. Grilled Steak with Spinach and Mushrooms

Prep Time: 5 minutes
Cook Time: 10 minutes
Servings: 1

Ingredients:

200g lean steak (such as sirloin)

1 tbsp olive oil

1/2 cup mushrooms, sliced

1/2 cup spinach, chopped

Salt and pepper to taste

Instructions:

Grill the steak to your desired doneness, about 4-5 minutes per side for medium-rare.

In a pan, heat olive oil over medium heat and sauté the mushrooms and spinach for 3-4 minutes until tender.

Slice the grilled steak and serve it alongside the spinach and mushrooms.

Why it's great:
This dish is packed with protein from the steak and spinach. It's a simple yet nutrient-dense lunch that combines rich flavours with high-quality protein.

## 10. Broccoli and Cheese Stuffed Chicken Breast

Prep Time: 10 minutes
Cook Time: 25 minutes
Servings: 1

Ingredients:

1 chicken breast

1/4 cup steamed broccoli, chopped

2 tbsp shredded cheddar cheese

1 tbsp olive oil

Salt and pepper to taste

Instructions:

Preheat the oven to 180°C (350°F).

Slice a pocket into the chicken breast, making sure not to cut all the way through.

Stuff the chicken breast with steamed broccoli and shredded cheese.

Season the chicken with salt and pepper, and drizzle with olive oil.

Bake for 20-25 minutes, or until the chicken is cooked through and the cheese is melted.

Why it's great:
This dish combines lean chicken with nutrient-rich broccoli and cheesy goodness. It's a filling, high-protein, low-carb meal that's perfect for lunch or dinner.

These high-protein, low-carb lunch recipes are designed to keep you satisfied while supporting your dietary goals. Whether you're craving a hearty salad, a grilled meal, or a comforting bowl, these recipes are sure to fuel your body with the nutrients it needs while keeping you on track with your healthy lifestyle.

## 11. Grilled Shrimp Salad with Lemon Vinaigrette

Prep Time: 10 minutes
Cook Time: 5 minutes
Servings: 1

Ingredients:

150g shrimp, peeled and deveined

1 tbsp olive oil

1/2 tsp garlic powder

1/2 tsp paprika

Salt and pepper to taste

1 cup mixed salad greens

1/4 cup cucumber, sliced

1/4 cup cherry tomatoes, halved

1 tbsp lemon juice

1 tbsp olive oil (for vinaigrette)

Instructions:

Preheat the grill or grill pan over medium-high heat.

Toss the shrimp with olive oil, garlic powder, paprika, salt, and pepper.

Grill the shrimp for 2-3 minutes on each side until pink and cooked through.

In a bowl, combine the mixed greens, cucumber, and cherry tomatoes.

Whisk together the lemon juice and olive oil for the vinaigrette and drizzle over the salad.

Top the salad with grilled shrimp and serve immediately.

Why it's great:
Shrimp is an excellent source of protein and low in fat, making it a perfect addition to your high-protein, low-carb lunch. The refreshing salad and tangy lemon vinaigrette complement the shrimp for a light but filling meal.

## 12. Chicken and Broccoli Stir-Fry

Prep Time: 10 minutes
Cook Time: 10 minutes
Servings: 1

Ingredients:

1 chicken breast, sliced into strips

1/2 cup broccoli florets

1/4 cup bell pepper, sliced

1/4 cup onion, sliced

1 tbsp olive oil

2 tbsp soy sauce (low-sodium)

1 tbsp rice vinegar

1/2 tsp sesame oil

1 tsp sesame seeds (optional)

Instructions:

Heat olive oil in a pan over medium heat. Add the chicken strips and cook for 5-6 minutes until browned and fully cooked.

Add the broccoli, bell pepper, and onion to the pan and sauté for 3-4 minutes until the vegetables are tender.

In a small bowl, whisk together the soy sauce, rice vinegar, and sesame oil.

Pour the sauce over the chicken and vegetables and stir to coat evenly.

Sprinkle with sesame seeds, if desired, and serve immediately.

Why it's great:
This stir-fry is loaded with protein from the chicken and fibre from the vegetables. The soy sauce and sesame oil give it a delicious savoury flavour while keeping the carbs low.

## 13. Spicy Chicken Lettuce Wraps

Prep Time: 10 minutes
Cook Time: 10 minutes
Servings: 2

Ingredients:

200g ground chicken

1 tbsp olive oil

1/4 cup red onion, finely chopped

1 tbsp chili sauce (optional)

1/2 tsp cumin

1/2 tsp paprika

Salt and pepper to taste

4-5 large lettuce leaves

1 tbsp cilantro, chopped (optional)

Instructions:

Heat olive oil in a pan over medium heat. Add the ground chicken and cook until browned, about 6-7 minutes.

Add the red onion, chili sauce (if using), cumin, paprika, salt, and pepper. Cook for another 2-3 minutes.

Spoon the chicken mixture into the centre of each lettuce leaf.

Garnish with chopped cilantro and serve immediately.

Why it's great:
These wraps are full of flavour and provide lean protein from the chicken. The lettuce wraps are a refreshing, low-carb alternative to tortillas, and the spices add an extra kick to this meal.

## 14. Grilled Turkey and Cheese Lettuce Wraps

Prep Time: 5 minutes
Cook Time: 5 minutes
Servings: 2

Ingredients:

100g sliced turkey breast

2 slices cheddar cheese (or your preferred cheese)

4 large lettuce leaves

1 tbsp mustard (optional)

Salt and pepper to taste

Instructions:

Lay the slices of turkey on a flat surface.

Place a slice of cheese on each turkey slice.

Fold the turkey around the cheese to form a wrap.

Lay each wrap in the centre of a large lettuce leaf and wrap it up like a burrito.

Serve with mustard if desired, and season with salt and pepper.

Why it's great:
These turkey and cheese wraps are low in carbs, high in protein, and quick to make. They are perfect for a satisfying and filling lunch when you're short on time but still want something nutritious.

## 15. Cauliflower Rice Stir-Fry with Chicken

Prep Time: 10 minutes
Cook Time: 10 minutes
Servings: 2

Ingredients:

200g chicken breast, diced

1 cup cauliflower rice (store-bought or homemade)

1/4 cup peas

1/4 cup carrots, chopped

2 tbsp soy sauce (low-sodium)

1 tbsp sesame oil

1/2 tsp garlic powder

1/4 tsp ginger powder

1 tbsp green onions, chopped (optional)

Instructions:

Heat sesame oil in a pan over medium heat. Add the diced chicken and cook until browned and fully cooked.

Add the peas and carrots to the pan and cook for 2-3 minutes.

Add the cauliflower rice to the pan and stir to combine. Cook for another 3-4 minutes until the cauliflower rice is tender.

Drizzle with soy sauce, and season with garlic and ginger powder.

Garnish with green onions, if desired, and serve immediately.

Why it's great:
This stir-fry is a delicious low-carb alternative to fried rice. The cauliflower rice provides the texture of rice without the carbs, while the chicken adds lean protein to keep you full.

## 16. Avocado Tuna Salad

Prep Time: 5 minutes
Cook Time: 0 minutes
Servings: 1

Ingredients:

1 can tuna (in olive oil or water), drained

1/2 avocado, mashed

1 tbsp mayonnaise (or Greek yogurt for a lighter version)

1 tbsp lemon juice

Salt and pepper to taste

1/4 cup celery, chopped (optional)

Instructions:

In a bowl, combine the tuna, mashed avocado, mayonnaise, and lemon juice.

Mix well and season with salt and pepper to taste.

Add chopped celery for extra crunch, if desired.

Serve immediately on its own or with lettuce wraps.

Why it's great:
This creamy tuna salad is high in protein and healthy fats from the avocado, making it a filling, low-carb lunch. It's quick, easy, and requires no cooking—perfect for a busy day.

## 17. Grilled Portobello Mushroom with Spinach and Cheese

Prep Time: 5 minutes
Cook Time: 10 minutes
Servings: 1

Ingredients:

2 large Portobello mushrooms, stems removed

1/4 cup spinach, sautéed

2 tbsp shredded mozzarella cheese

1 tbsp olive oil

Salt and pepper to taste

Instructions:

Preheat the grill or grill pan to medium heat.

Brush the Portobello mushrooms with olive oil and season with salt and pepper.

Grill the mushrooms for 4-5 minutes per side, or until tender.

Top the grilled mushrooms with sautéed spinach and mozzarella cheese.

Grill for an additional 1-2 minutes until the cheese is melted. Serve immediately.

Why it's great:
Portobello mushrooms make an excellent low-carb base for this meal, providing a hearty texture. Combined with spinach and cheese, this dish is a perfect vegetarian-friendly, high-protein lunch.

## 18. Chicken Caesar Salad (Without the Croutons)

Prep Time: 10 minutes
Cook Time: 10 minutes
Servings: 1

Ingredients:

1 chicken breast, grilled and sliced

2 cups romaine lettuce, chopped

2 tbsp Caesar dressing (look for a low-carb version)

1 tbsp grated Parmesan cheese

Salt and pepper to taste

Instructions:

Grill the chicken breast until fully cooked, about 6-7 minutes per side.

Slice the chicken and set it aside.

In a bowl, combine the chopped lettuce with the Caesar dressing and toss well.

Top with the grilled chicken and grated Parmesan cheese.

Season with salt and pepper to taste, and serve immediately.

Why it's great:
This Caesar salad is a great way to enjoy a classic without the carbs from croutons. Grilled chicken adds lean protein, while the dressing and Parmesan bring rich flavours to this satisfying, low-carb meal.

## 19. Grilled Chicken and Pesto Zoodles

Prep Time: 10 minutes
Cook Time: 10 minutes
Servings: 1

Ingredients:

1 chicken breast, grilled and sliced

1 medium zucchini, spiralised into noodles (zoodles)

2 tbsp homemade or store-bought pesto

1 tbsp olive oil

Salt and pepper to taste

1 tbsp Parmesan cheese (optional)

Instructions:

Grill the chicken breast until fully cooked, about 6-7 minutes per side. Slice it thinly.

In a pan, heat olive oil over medium heat. Add the zoodles and sauté for 2-3 minutes until tender.

Toss the zoodles with the pesto, ensuring they're well-coated.

Top with the sliced grilled chicken and sprinkle with Parmesan cheese if desired.

Serve immediately.

Why it's great:
This recipe replaces traditional pasta with zucchini noodles, which are low in carbs but high in nutrients. The pesto adds healthy fats and a burst of flavour, while the grilled chicken provides lean protein.

## 20. Beef and Vegetable Stir-Fry

Prep Time: 10 minutes
Cook Time: 10 minutes
Servings: 1

Ingredients:

150g lean beef, thinly sliced

1/4 cup bell pepper, sliced

1/4 cup broccoli florets

1/4 cup onions, sliced

1 tbsp olive oil

2 tbsp soy sauce (low-sodium)

1 tsp sesame oil (optional)

1 tsp grated ginger (optional)

Instructions:

Heat olive oil in a pan over medium-high heat. Add the beef and cook for 4-5 minutes, stirring occasionally.

Add the bell pepper, broccoli, and onions, and cook for another 3-4 minutes until the vegetables are tender.

Stir in soy sauce, sesame oil (if using), and grated ginger.

Cook for another 1-2 minutes, then remove from heat and serve.

Why it's great:
This stir-fry is packed with protein from the lean beef and fibre from the vegetables. The soy sauce and sesame oil add a savoury depth of flavour, making this a quick, satisfying lunch.

## 21. Chicken, Cucumber, and Hummus Bowl

Prep Time: 10 minutes
Cook Time: 0 minutes
Servings: 1

Ingredients:

1 grilled chicken breast, sliced

1/2 cucumber, sliced

2 tbsp hummus

1 tbsp olive oil

1 tbsp lemon juice

Salt and pepper to taste

Instructions:

Grill the chicken breast until fully cooked, about 6-7 minutes per side. Slice thinly.

In a bowl, combine the cucumber slices and drizzle with olive oil and lemon juice.

Top the cucumber with the grilled chicken and a generous scoop of hummus.

Season with salt and pepper to taste and serve immediately.

Why it's great:
This is a light yet filling lunch that combines lean protein from the chicken with the creamy, nutrient-dense hummus. The cucumber adds a refreshing crunch, while the olive oil and lemon juice provide healthy fats and a bright flavour.

## 22. Shrimp and Avocado Salad with Lime Dressing

Prep Time: 10 minutes
Cook Time: 5 minutes
Servings: 1

Ingredients:

150g shrimp, peeled and deveined

1/2 avocado, diced

1 cup mixed salad greens

1 tbsp lime juice

1 tbsp olive oil

Salt and pepper to taste

Instructions:

Heat a pan over medium heat and cook the shrimp for 2-3 minutes per side, or until pink and fully cooked.

In a bowl, combine the mixed greens, avocado, and cooked shrimp.

Drizzle with lime juice and olive oil, and toss gently to combine.

Season with salt and pepper to taste, and serve immediately.

Why it's great:
Shrimp is a great source of lean protein, while avocado provides healthy fats and fibre. This light yet satisfying salad is perfect for a low-carb lunch, and the lime dressing adds a tangy, refreshing flavour.

## 23. Baked Salmon with Asparagus and Lemon

Prep Time: 5 minutes
Cook Time: 20 minutes
Servings: 1

Ingredients:

1 salmon fillet

1/2 bunch asparagus, trimmed

1 tbsp olive oil

1 tbsp lemon juice

1/2 tsp garlic powder

Salt and pepper to taste

Instructions:

Preheat your oven to 200°C (400°F).

Place the salmon fillet and asparagus on a baking tray.

Drizzle with olive oil and lemon juice, and season with garlic powder, salt, and pepper.

Bake for 18-20 minutes, or until the salmon is cooked through and flakes easily with a fork.

Serve immediately.

Why it's great:
Salmon is a rich source of omega-3 fatty acids and protein, while asparagus provides fibre and antioxidants. This simple dish is packed with nutrients and is perfect for a quick, healthy lunch.

## 24. Chicken and Avocado Lettuce Wraps

Prep Time: 10 minutes
Cook Time: 10 minutes
Servings: 2

Ingredients:

200g chicken breast, grilled and shredded

1 avocado, diced

4 large lettuce leaves (romaine or butter lettuce)

1 tbsp fresh cilantro, chopped

1 tbsp lime juice

Salt and pepper to taste

Instructions:

Grill the chicken breast until fully cooked, about 6-7 minutes per side. Shred the chicken using two forks.

In a bowl, combine the shredded chicken, diced avocado, cilantro, and lime juice.

Season with salt and pepper to taste and mix gently.

Spoon the chicken and avocado mixture onto the centre of each lettuce leaf.

Wrap the lettuce leaves around the filling and serve immediately.

Why it's great:
These lettuce wraps are low in carbs but high in protein and healthy fats. The avocado adds a creamy texture, and the cilantro and lime juice bring a fresh, tangy flavour to this quick, satisfying meal.

## 25. Cauliflower Rice and Chicken Stir-Fry

Prep Time: 10 minutes
Cook Time: 10 minutes
Servings: 2

Ingredients:

200g chicken breast, diced

1 cup cauliflower rice (fresh or frozen)

1/4 cup bell pepper, chopped

1/4 cup onion, chopped

2 tbsp soy sauce (low-sodium)

1 tbsp olive oil

Salt and pepper to taste

Instructions:

Heat olive oil in a pan over medium-high heat. Add the diced chicken and cook for 5-6 minutes until browned and fully cooked.

Add the bell pepper and onion to the pan, and sauté for 2-3 minutes until softened.

Stir in the cauliflower rice and soy sauce, and cook for another 3-4 minutes until the rice is tender.

Season with salt and pepper to taste, and serve immediately.

Why it's great:
Cauliflower rice is a fantastic low-carb alternative to regular rice. Combined with lean chicken and vegetables, this stir-fry provides a nutrient-packed, filling lunch that supports fat loss and muscle growth.

# Chapter 4: Dinner Recipes

### Overview of a High-Protein Dinner

Dinner is an essential opportunity to nourish your body with high-quality protein and healthy fats, while keeping carbs to a minimum. A high-protein, low-carb dinner ensures that your body continues to repair muscles, maintain metabolic health, and burn fat efficiently overnight. Since dinner tends to be a larger meal, it's important to focus on nutrient-dense options that will fuel you for the rest of the evening and leave you feeling satisfied.

Protein is vital for muscle recovery and growth, making it an important focus of your dinner. Low-carb vegetables provide fibre, vitamins, and minerals, while healthy fats keep you full and support overall health. This chapter includes 20 delicious, high-protein, low-carb dinner recipes that are easy to prepare and packed with nutrients to keep you on track with your health and fitness goals.

## 1. Baked Salmon with Lemon and Asparagus

Prep Time: 5 minutes
Cook Time: 20 minutes
Servings: 1

Ingredients:

1 salmon fillet

1/2 bunch asparagus, trimmed

1 tbsp olive oil

1 tbsp lemon juice

Salt and pepper to taste

1/4 tsp garlic powder (optional)

Instructions:

Preheat the oven to 200°C (400°F).

Place the salmon fillet and asparagus on a baking tray. Drizzle with olive oil and lemon juice.

Season with salt, pepper, and garlic powder, if using.

Bake for 18-20 minutes or until the salmon is cooked through and flakes easily with a fork.

Serve immediately.

Why it's great:
Salmon is rich in protein and healthy omega-3 fatty acids. Asparagus is a low-carb vegetable that provides fibre and antioxidants, making this dish a balanced and nutritious dinner.

## 2. Chicken and Veggie Stir-Fry with Soy Sauce

Prep Time: 10 minutes
Cook Time: 10 minutes
Servings: 1

Ingredients:

200g chicken breast, sliced into strips

1/2 cup broccoli florets

1/4 cup bell pepper, sliced

1/4 cup carrots, julienned

2 tbsp soy sauce (low-sodium)

1 tbsp olive oil

1 tsp sesame oil (optional)

Salt and pepper to taste

Instructions:

Heat olive oil in a pan over medium heat. Add the chicken strips and cook for 6-7 minutes, or until browned and fully cooked.

Add the broccoli, bell pepper, and carrots to the pan and stir-fry for another 3-4 minutes until the vegetables are tender.

Stir in the soy sauce and sesame oil, then cook for another minute.

Season with salt and pepper to taste, and serve immediately.

Why it's great:
This stir-fry is loaded with lean protein from the chicken and fibre from the vegetables. The soy sauce and sesame oil add a savoury, umami flavour, making this an easy, satisfying dinner.

## 3. Grilled Steak with Garlic Butter and Veggies

Prep Time: 5 minutes
Cook Time: 10 minutes
Servings: 1

Ingredients:

200g sirloin steak

1 tbsp olive oil

2 tbsp unsalted butter

1 garlic clove, minced

1/4 cup mushrooms, sliced

1/4 cup spinach, chopped

Salt and pepper to taste

Instructions:

Preheat the grill or grill pan over medium-high heat.

Rub the steak with olive oil and season with salt and pepper.

Grill the steak for 4-5 minutes per side for medium-rare, or longer if desired.

In a small pan, melt the butter and sauté the garlic until fragrant (about 1 minute). Add the mushrooms and spinach, cooking until tender.

Serve the grilled steak with the garlic butter mushrooms and spinach on the side.

Why it's great:
Steak is a great source of protein and iron, while garlic butter adds rich flavour to the meal. The mushrooms and spinach provide antioxidants and fibre, making this a satisfying dinner option.

## 4. Stuffed Bell Peppers with Ground Turkey

Prep Time: 10 minutes
Cook Time: 25 minutes
Servings: 2

Ingredients:

2 large bell peppers, tops cut off and seeds removed

200g ground turkey

1/4 cup onion, chopped

1/4 cup spinach, chopped

1/2 cup shredded mozzarella cheese

1/2 tsp garlic powder

1/4 tsp cumin

Salt and pepper to taste

Instructions:

Preheat the oven to 180°C (350°F).

In a pan, cook the ground turkey with chopped onion over medium heat until browned, about 5-6 minutes.

Add the spinach, garlic powder, cumin, salt, and pepper to the pan, cooking for another 2-3 minutes until the spinach wilts.

Stuff the bell peppers with the turkey mixture and place them on a baking tray.

Top each stuffed pepper with shredded mozzarella cheese.

Bake for 20-25 minutes, or until the peppers are tender and the cheese is melted.

Serve immediately.

Why it's great:
This recipe is a low-carb alternative to traditional stuffed peppers, using ground turkey as a lean source of protein. The mozzarella cheese adds richness, while the spinach provides a nutrient boost.

## 5. Cauliflower Rice with Shrimp

Prep Time: 5 minutes
Cook Time: 10 minutes
Servings: 1

Ingredients:

150g shrimp, peeled and deveined

1 cup cauliflower rice (store-bought or homemade)

1/4 cup bell pepper, diced

1/4 cup onion, diced

1 tbsp olive oil

1 tbsp soy sauce (low-sodium)

1/2 tsp garlic powder

Salt and pepper to taste

Instructions:

Heat olive oil in a pan over medium heat. Add the shrimp and cook for 2-3 minutes per side until pink and fully cooked.

Remove the shrimp from the pan and set aside.

In the same pan, sauté the bell pepper and onion for 2-3 minutes until softened.

Add the cauliflower rice to the pan and cook for another 3-4 minutes, stirring frequently.

Stir in the soy sauce, garlic powder, salt, and pepper. Add the cooked shrimp back to the pan and toss everything together.

Serve immediately.

Why it's great:
This dish is a low-carb alternative to traditional fried rice. The shrimp provides a high-protein boost, while cauliflower rice offers a fibre-packed base without the carbs. It's a quick, healthy meal that's full of flavour.

## 6. Zucchini Lasagna with Ground Beef

Prep Time: 10 minutes
Cook Time: 25 minutes
Servings: 2

Ingredients:

2 medium zucchinis, sliced lengthwise into thin strips

200g ground beef

1/4 cup onion, chopped

1/2 cup marinara sauce (low-carb)

1/4 cup ricotta cheese

1/2 cup shredded mozzarella cheese

1 tbsp olive oil

Salt and pepper to taste

Instructions:

Preheat the oven to 180°C (350°F).

In a pan, cook the ground beef with chopped onion over medium heat until browned, about 5-6 minutes. Drain any excess fat.

Add marinara sauce to the beef and cook for an additional 2-3 minutes, seasoning with salt and pepper.

In a baking dish, layer the zucchini slices, ground beef mixture, and ricotta cheese. Repeat layers until all ingredients are used.

Top with shredded mozzarella cheese.

Bake for 20-25 minutes until the cheese is melted and bubbly.

Serve immediately.

Why it's great:
This zucchini lasagna is a low-carb alternative to traditional pasta lasagna. The zucchini provides the texture of noodles, while the ground beef and cheese add protein and richness to this satisfying dish.

## 7. Cilantro-Lime Chicken with Roasted Vegetables

Prep Time: 10 minutes
Cook Time: 25 minutes
Servings: 1

Ingredients:

1 chicken breast

1 tbsp olive oil

1 tbsp lime juice

1 tbsp cilantro, chopped

1/2 cup bell pepper, chopped

1/2 cup zucchini, chopped

1/4 cup red onion, chopped

Salt and pepper to taste

Instructions:

Preheat the oven to 200°C (400°F).

Rub the chicken breast with olive oil, lime juice, cilantro, salt, and pepper.

Arrange the chopped vegetables on a baking tray and drizzle with olive oil.

Roast the vegetables in the oven for 20-25 minutes, stirring halfway through.

Meanwhile, grill or pan-sear the chicken for 6-7 minutes per side until fully cooked.

Serve the grilled chicken with roasted vegetables.

Why it's great:
This dish is full of flavour, with fresh cilantro and lime enhancing the chicken and vegetables. It's a high-protein, low-carb meal that's packed with vitamins and minerals, making it perfect for dinner.

## 8. Grilled Shrimp Skewers with Cauliflower Rice

Prep Time: 10 minutes
Cook Time: 10 minutes
Servings: 2

Ingredients:

200g shrimp, peeled and deveined

1 tbsp olive oil

1 tsp paprika

1/2 tsp garlic powder

Salt and pepper to taste

1 cup cauliflower rice (store-bought or homemade)

1 tbsp olive oil (for cauliflower rice)

1/4 cup parsley, chopped

Lemon wedges for garnish

Instructions:

Preheat the grill or grill pan over medium-high heat.

In a bowl, toss the shrimp with olive oil, paprika, garlic powder, salt, and pepper.

Thread the shrimp onto skewers and grill for 2-3 minutes per side, until cooked through.

In a pan, heat olive oil over medium heat and sauté the cauliflower rice for 3-4 minutes until tender.

Top the cauliflower rice with the grilled shrimp skewers and garnish with chopped parsley and lemon wedges.

Serve immediately.

Why it's great:
Shrimp is a lean source of protein and pairs perfectly with cauliflower rice as a low-carb alternative to traditional rice. This dish is quick, easy, and perfect for a light yet satisfying dinner.

## 9. Spaghetti Squash with Marinara and Turkey Meatballs

Prep Time: 10 minutes
Cook Time: 30 minutes
Servings: 2

Ingredients:

1 medium spaghetti squash

200g ground turkey

1/4 cup almond flour

1/4 tsp garlic powder

1/4 tsp onion powder

Salt and pepper to taste

1/2 cup marinara sauce (low-carb)

1/4 cup shredded Parmesan cheese

Instructions:

Preheat the oven to 200°C (400°F).

Cut the spaghetti squash in half lengthwise and remove the seeds. Place the halves on a baking tray and roast for 25-30 minutes until tender.

Meanwhile, mix the ground turkey with almond flour, garlic powder, onion powder, salt, and pepper. Form the mixture into meatballs.

Heat a pan over medium heat and cook the turkey meatballs for 8-10 minutes, until fully cooked.

Once the squash is roasted, use a fork to scrape out the spaghetti-like strands and place them in a bowl.

Heat the marinara sauce in a pan and pour over the squash strands.

Top with turkey meatballs and shredded Parmesan cheese. Serve immediately.

Why it's great:
Spaghetti squash is a fantastic low-carb pasta substitute. Combined with lean turkey meatballs and marinara sauce, this dish offers a satisfying and hearty meal while keeping carbs in check.

## 10. Grilled Portobello Mushrooms with Goat Cheese

Prep Time: 5 minutes
Cook Time: 10 minutes
Servings: 1

**Ingredients:**

2 large Portobello mushrooms, stems removed

1 tbsp olive oil

2 tbsp goat cheese, crumbled

1 tbsp balsamic vinegar

Salt and pepper to taste

Fresh basil for garnish (optional)

Instructions:

Preheat the grill or grill pan over medium-high heat.

Brush the Portobello mushrooms with olive oil and season with salt and pepper.

Grill the mushrooms for 4-5 minutes on each side, or until tender.

Top the grilled mushrooms with crumbled goat cheese and drizzle with balsamic vinegar.

Garnish with fresh basil, if desired, and serve immediately.

Why it's great:
Portobello mushrooms are a great low-carb alternative to meat and provide a meaty texture. Topped with tangy goat cheese, they make for a rich, satisfying, and healthy dinner.

## 11. Lemon Herb Chicken with Roasted Brussels Sprouts

Prep Time: 10 minutes
Cook Time: 25 minutes
Servings: 2

Ingredients:

2 chicken breasts

1 tbsp olive oil

1 tbsp lemon juice

1/2 tsp dried thyme

1/2 tsp garlic powder

Salt and pepper to taste

1 cup Brussels sprouts, halved

1 tbsp olive oil (for roasting Brussels sprouts)

Instructions:

Preheat the oven to 200°C (400°F).

Rub the chicken breasts with olive oil, lemon juice, dried thyme, garlic powder, salt, and pepper.

Place the chicken breasts on a baking tray and roast for 20-25 minutes until fully cooked.

Toss the Brussels sprouts with olive oil, salt, and pepper, and roast for 20-25 minutes, shaking the tray halfway through, until crispy and golden.

Serve the chicken alongside the roasted Brussels sprouts.

Why it's great:
This dish is a balanced, nutrient-dense meal with lean protein from the chicken and plenty of fibre and vitamins from the Brussels sprouts. The lemon and herbs add a fresh, aromatic flavour.

## 12. Baked Cod with Roasted Vegetables

Prep Time: 5 minutes
Cook Time: 20 minutes
Servings: 1

Ingredients:

1 cod fillet

1 tbsp olive oil

1/4 tsp garlic powder

Salt and pepper to taste

1/2 cup cauliflower, chopped

1/2 cup broccoli florets

1 tbsp olive oil (for vegetables)

Instructions:

Preheat the oven to 200°C (400°F).

Place the cod fillet on a baking tray and drizzle with olive oil. Season with garlic powder, salt, and pepper.

On the same tray, add the cauliflower and broccoli. Drizzle with olive oil and season with salt and pepper.

Bake for 18-20 minutes, or until the cod is cooked through and flakes easily with a fork, and the vegetables are tender.

Serve immediately.

Why it's great:
Cod is a lean fish rich in protein and low in fat. Paired with fibre-rich roasted vegetables, this dish is light yet filling, providing a complete, nutrient-packed dinner.

## 13. Chicken and Spinach Stuffed Sweet Potatoes

Prep Time: 10 minutes
Cook Time: 30 minutes
Servings: 2

Ingredients:

2 medium sweet potatoes

200g chicken breast, cooked and shredded

1/2 cup spinach, chopped

1/4 cup Greek yogurt

1 tbsp olive oil

Salt and pepper to taste

Instructions:

Preheat the oven to 200°C (400°F).

Pierce the sweet potatoes with a fork and bake for 25-30 minutes, until soft.

While the potatoes are baking, heat olive oil in a pan and sauté the spinach until wilted.

Once the sweet potatoes are done, cut them open and scoop out some of the flesh.

Mix the shredded chicken, sautéed spinach, and Greek yogurt, then stuff the mixture into the sweet potatoes.

Return the stuffed sweet potatoes to the oven for an additional 5 minutes, then serve.

Why it's great:
Sweet potatoes provide complex carbs and fibre, making this dish a great option for a well-rounded dinner. The chicken and spinach filling adds lean protein and essential nutrients, while Greek yogurt contributes creaminess and a protein boost.

## 14. Eggplant Parmesan (Low-Carb Version)

Prep Time: 10 minutes
Cook Time: 25 minutes
Servings: 2

Ingredients:

2 small eggplants, sliced into rounds

1 egg, beaten

1/2 cup almond flour

1/2 cup grated Parmesan cheese

1/2 cup marinara sauce (low-carb)

1/2 cup shredded mozzarella cheese

1 tbsp olive oil

Instructions:

Preheat the oven to 180°C (350°F).

Dip the eggplant slices in the beaten egg, then coat in a mixture of almond flour and Parmesan cheese.

Arrange the eggplant slices on a baking tray and drizzle with olive oil. Bake for 20-25 minutes until golden brown.

Top each slice with marinara sauce and shredded mozzarella cheese.

Return to the oven for another 5 minutes, or until the cheese is melted and bubbly.

Serve immediately.

Why it's great:
This low-carb version of eggplant Parmesan is a great way to enjoy a comforting, cheesy meal without the carbs from breadcrumbs or pasta. The almond flour coating provides a crunchy texture, while the mozzarella adds richness.

## 15. Beef and Broccoli Stir-Fry

Prep Time: 10 minutes
Cook Time: 10 minutes
Servings: 2

Ingredients:

200g lean beef, thinly sliced

1 cup broccoli florets

1 tbsp olive oil

2 tbsp soy sauce (low-sodium)

1 tbsp rice vinegar

1/4 tsp garlic powder

Salt and pepper to taste

Instructions:

Heat olive oil in a pan over medium-high heat. Add the beef and cook for 4-5 minutes, or until browned.

Add the broccoli florets to the pan and stir-fry for another 3-4 minutes until the broccoli is tender but still crisp.

Stir in soy sauce, rice vinegar, garlic powder, salt, and pepper.

Cook for an additional minute until the sauce is well-combined and the beef is fully cooked.

Serve immediately.

Why it's great:
This stir-fry is a quick and satisfying dinner. Beef provides a rich source of protein and iron, while broccoli offers fibre and vitamins. The soy sauce adds a savoury depth of flavour, making this a delicious, balanced meal.

## 16. Spicy Baked Chicken with Avocado Salsa

Prep Time: 10 minutes
Cook Time: 30 minutes
Servings: 2

Ingredients:

2 chicken breasts

1 tbsp olive oil

1 tsp smoked paprika

1/2 tsp chili powder

1/4 tsp cayenne pepper (optional)

Salt and pepper to taste

1 ripe avocado, diced

1/4 cup red onion, finely chopped

1 tbsp lime juice

1 tbsp fresh cilantro, chopped

Instructions:

Preheat the oven to 200°C (400°F).

Rub the chicken breasts with olive oil, smoked paprika, chili powder, cayenne pepper, salt, and pepper.

Place the chicken breasts on a baking tray and bake for 25-30 minutes until fully cooked.

While the chicken is baking, combine the avocado, red onion, lime juice, and cilantro in a bowl. Mix gently to make the salsa.

Once the chicken is done, serve it with a generous scoop of avocado salsa on top.

Why it's great:
This dish is packed with protein from the chicken and healthy fats from the avocado. The spicy seasoning adds bold flavours, while the refreshing salsa provides a cooling contrast, making it the perfect dinner combination.

## 17. Grilled Chicken and Cucumber Salad

Prep Time: 10 minutes
Cook Time: 10 minutes
Servings: 2

Ingredients:

2 chicken breasts

1 tbsp olive oil

Salt and pepper to taste

1/2 cucumber, thinly sliced

1/4 cup red onion, thinly sliced

1/4 cup feta cheese, crumbled

2 tbsp olive oil (for dressing)

1 tbsp red wine vinegar

1 tbsp lemon juice

Instructions:

Preheat the grill or grill pan over medium-high heat.

Rub the chicken breasts with olive oil and season with salt and pepper. Grill for 5-6 minutes per side, or until fully cooked.

While the chicken is grilling, prepare the salad by combining the cucumber, red onion, and feta cheese in a bowl.

Whisk together the olive oil, red wine vinegar, and lemon juice for the dressing.

Once the chicken is cooked, slice it and add it to the salad. Drizzle the dressing over the top and serve immediately.

Why it's great:
Grilled chicken provides a lean source of protein, while the cucumber and red onion add a fresh, crunchy texture. The feta cheese and dressing add a creamy and tangy flavour to this simple, satisfying meal.

## 18. Roasted Lemon Herb Chicken with Green Beans

Prep Time: 10 minutes
Cook Time: 30 minutes
Servings: 2

Ingredients:

2 chicken breasts

1 tbsp olive oil

1 tbsp lemon juice

1 tsp dried rosemary

1/2 tsp garlic powder

Salt and pepper to taste

1 cup green beans, trimmed

Instructions:

Preheat the oven to 200°C (400°F).

Rub the chicken breasts with olive oil, lemon juice, rosemary, garlic powder, salt, and pepper.

Place the chicken breasts on a baking tray and bake for 25-30 minutes, or until fully cooked.

While the chicken is baking, steam or sauté the green beans until tender.

Serve the roasted chicken alongside the green beans.

Why it's great:
This dinner combines lean chicken with antioxidant-rich green beans. The lemon and rosemary add aromatic flavours, while the green beans provide fibre, making this a light but nourishing meal.

## 19. Grilled Pork Chops with Brussels Sprouts

Prep Time: 10 minutes
Cook Time: 15 minutes
Servings: 2

Ingredients:

2 pork chops

1 tbsp olive oil

1 tsp garlic powder

1/2 tsp smoked paprika

Salt and pepper to taste

1 cup Brussels sprouts, halved

1 tbsp olive oil (for Brussels sprouts)

Instructions:

Preheat the grill or grill pan over medium-high heat.

Rub the pork chops with olive oil, garlic powder, smoked paprika, salt, and pepper.

Grill the pork chops for 6-7 minutes on each side, or until fully cooked.

Meanwhile, heat olive oil in a pan over medium heat and sauté the Brussels sprouts until crispy and golden, about 7-8 minutes.

Serve the grilled pork chops alongside the sautéed Brussels sprouts.

Why it's great:
Pork chops are a great source of protein, and when paired with fibre-packed Brussels sprouts, this meal becomes a filling yet low-carb dinner option. The smoky paprika enhances the flavour of the pork, while the Brussels sprouts add a healthy crunch.

## 20. Eggplant and Ground Turkey Stir-Fry

Prep Time: 10 minutes
Cook Time: 10 minutes
Servings: 2

Ingredients:

200g ground turkey

1 medium eggplant, diced

1/4 cup onion, chopped

1 tbsp olive oil

2 tbsp soy sauce (low-sodium)

1 tsp garlic powder

Salt and pepper to taste

Instructions:

Heat olive oil in a pan over medium heat. Add the ground turkey and cook until browned, about 5-6 minutes.

Add the onion and eggplant to the pan and sauté for 3-4 minutes, or until the eggplant becomes tender.

Stir in soy sauce, garlic powder, salt, and pepper, and cook for another 2-3 minutes.

Serve immediately.

Why it's great:
This stir-fry is a quick and healthy dinner packed with lean protein from the turkey and plenty of vegetables. The eggplant provides a satisfying texture, while the soy sauce adds a savory depth of flavour to the dish.

## 21. Baked Chicken Thighs with Cauliflower Mash

Prep Time: 10 minutes
Cook Time: 30 minutes
Servings: 2

Ingredients:

2 chicken thighs, bone-in and skin-on

1 tbsp olive oil

1 tsp paprika

1/2 tsp garlic powder

Salt and pepper to taste

1 cup cauliflower florets

1 tbsp butter (optional)

Instructions:

Preheat the oven to 200°C (400°F).

Rub the chicken thighs with olive oil, paprika, garlic powder, salt, and pepper.

Place the chicken thighs on a baking tray and bake for 25-30 minutes, or until fully cooked.

While the chicken is baking, steam the cauliflower florets until tender.

Mash the cauliflower with a fork or in a food processor, adding butter if desired for a creamy texture.

Serve the baked chicken thighs with cauliflower mash.

Why it's great:
Chicken thighs are juicy and full of flavour, while the cauliflower mash is a perfect low-carb substitute for mashed potatoes. This dish is a comforting and satisfying meal that fits perfectly into a high-protein, low-carb lifestyle.

# Chapter 5: Snacks & Sides

## Overview of High-Protein, Low-Carb Snacks

Snacking is an essential part of maintaining energy levels throughout the day, especially when following a high-protein, low-carb diet. Choosing the right snacks can help you stay on track with your nutrition goals without reaching for unhealthy, sugar-laden options. High-protein, low-carb snacks are designed to fuel your body, support muscle recovery, and keep you feeling full between meals, all while keeping carbs to a minimum.

These snacks are not only easy and quick to prepare but also highly satisfying, ensuring that you stay on top of your goals. Whether you need a post-workout snack, something to munch on during the afternoon slump, or a healthy side to complement your meal, this chapter provides a wide range of options that support both your cravings and dietary needs.

## 1. Hard-Boiled Eggs with Salt and Pepper

Prep Time: 5 minutes
Cook Time: 10 minutes
Servings: 1

Ingredients:

2 large eggs

Salt and pepper to taste

Instructions:

Place the eggs in a saucepan and cover with water. Bring to a boil over medium-high heat.

Once the water starts boiling, reduce the heat and simmer for 9-10 minutes.

Remove the eggs and cool under cold running water or in an ice bath.

Peel the eggs and sprinkle with salt and pepper to taste.

Serve immediately.

Why it's great:
Hard-boiled eggs are a perfect on-the-go snack, rich in protein and healthy fats. They are quick to make, filling, and provide essential nutrients to keep you going through the day.

## 2. Crispy Roasted Chickpeas

Prep Time: 5 minutes
Cook Time: 30 minutes
Servings: 2

Ingredients:

1 can chickpeas, drained and rinsed

1 tbsp olive oil

1/2 tsp paprika

1/2 tsp garlic powder

Salt to taste

Instructions:

Preheat the oven to 200°C (400°F).

Pat the chickpeas dry with a paper towel.

Toss the chickpeas with olive oil, paprika, garlic powder, and salt.

Spread the chickpeas evenly on a baking sheet.

Roast for 25-30 minutes, stirring halfway through, until golden and crispy.

Serve immediately.

Why it's great:
Roasted chickpeas are a high-fibre, protein-packed snack that provides a satisfying crunch. The seasoning adds flavour, making it a delicious low-carb alternative to traditional chips.

## 3. Avocado and Tuna Bites

Prep Time: 5 minutes
Cook Time: 0 minutes
Servings: 1

Ingredients:

1/2 avocado, sliced

1 can tuna in olive oil, drained

1 tbsp lemon juice

Salt and pepper to taste

Instructions:

Scoop the tuna into a bowl and mix with lemon juice, salt, and pepper.

Place a spoonful of the tuna mixture on each slice of avocado.

Serve immediately.

Why it's great:
This snack combines the healthy fats from avocado with protein from tuna. It's a simple, no-cook snack that provides essential nutrients and keeps you full for hours.

## 4. Greek Yogurt with Flaxseeds and Almonds

Prep Time: 2 minutes
Cook Time: 0 minutes
Servings: 1

Ingredients:

1/2 cup plain Greek yogurt (unsweetened)

1 tbsp ground flaxseeds

1 tbsp sliced almonds

Stevia or honey (optional)

Instructions:

Scoop the Greek yogurt into a bowl.

Top with ground flaxseeds and sliced almonds.

Add sweetener if desired, and stir to combine.

Serve immediately.

Why it's great:
Greek yogurt is high in protein and probiotics, while flaxseeds and almonds provide fibre and healthy fats. This snack supports digestion and keeps you full, making it a great choice for a mid-afternoon pick-me-up.

## 5. Cheese and Cucumber Bites

Prep Time: 5 minutes
Cook Time: 0 minutes
Servings: 2

Ingredients:

1/2 cucumber, sliced

2 oz cheese (cheddar, mozzarella, or your choice), sliced

Instructions:

Slice the cucumber into rounds.

Place a slice of cheese on each cucumber round.

Serve immediately.

Why it's great:
These cheese and cucumber bites are a refreshing and filling snack. The cheese provides protein and healthy fats, while the cucumber adds a hydrating crunch with minimal carbs.

## 6. Roasted Almonds with Sea Salt

Prep Time: 5 minutes
Cook Time: 15 minutes
Servings: 2

Ingredients:

1 cup raw almonds

1 tbsp olive oil

Sea salt to taste

Instructions:

Preheat the oven to 180°C (350°F).

Toss the almonds with olive oil and sea salt.

Spread the almonds evenly on a baking sheet.

Roast for 12-15 minutes, stirring halfway through, until golden and fragrant.

Serve immediately.

Why it's great:
Roasted almonds are a nutrient-dense snack full of healthy fats and protein. The sea salt adds a savoury touch, making them a satisfying snack that is both delicious and filling.

## 7. Veggie Sticks with Hummus

Prep Time: 5 minutes
Cook Time: 0 minutes
Servings: 1

Ingredients:

1/2 cucumber, sliced into sticks

1/2 carrot, sliced into sticks

1/4 bell pepper, sliced into sticks

1/4 cup hummus

Instructions:

Arrange the veggie sticks on a plate.

Serve with hummus for dipping.

Why it's great:
This snack is full of fibre and protein. The veggies provide crunch and hydration, while the hummus offers a creamy dip rich in healthy fats and protein. It's a perfect low-carb snack that's both satisfying and healthy.

## 8. Roasted Pumpkin Seeds

Prep Time: 5 minutes
Cook Time: 15 minutes
Servings: 2

Ingredients:

1 cup pumpkin seeds

1 tbsp olive oil

Salt to taste

1/4 tsp paprika (optional)

Instructions:

Preheat the oven to 180°C (350°F).

Toss the pumpkin seeds with olive oil, salt, and paprika.

Spread the seeds evenly on a baking sheet.

Roast for 12-15 minutes, stirring halfway through, until golden and crispy.

Serve immediately.

Why it's great:
Pumpkin seeds are a great source of protein, healthy fats, and zinc. This simple snack is easy to prepare, and the roasted seeds are both crunchy and satisfying.

## 9. Cheese-Stuffed Olives

**Prep Time:** 5 minutes
**Cook Time:** 0 minutes
**Servings:** 1

Ingredients:

8-10 green or black olives, pitted

1 oz cream cheese or goat cheese

Instructions:

Stuff each olive with a small amount of cream cheese or goat cheese.

Serve immediately.

Why it's great:
Olives are high in healthy fats, and the cheese adds a creamy protein boost. This snack is both satisfying and simple, perfect for a quick bite that keeps you on track with your low-carb goals.

## 10. Mini Quinoa Bites

**Prep Time:** 5 minutes
**Cook Time:** 25 minutes
**Servings:** 2

Ingredients:

1/2 cup cooked quinoa

1 egg

1/4 cup grated Parmesan cheese

1/4 tsp garlic powder

Salt and pepper to taste

1 tbsp olive oil (for greasing)

Instructions:

Preheat the oven to 180°C (350°F). Grease a mini muffin tin with olive oil.

In a bowl, mix the cooked quinoa, egg, Parmesan cheese, garlic powder, salt, and pepper.

Spoon the mixture into the mini muffin tin, pressing down lightly.

Bake for 20-25 minutes, or until golden brown.

Serve immediately.

Why it's great:
These mini quinoa bites are a protein-packed, low-carb snack with a crispy exterior and a cheesy interior. They're great for meal prep and make an excellent snack or side dish.

## 11. Edamame with Sea Salt

**Prep Time:** 5 minutes

Cook Time: 5 minutes
Servings: 1

Ingredients:

1 cup edamame (fresh or frozen)

Sea salt to taste

Instructions:

Bring a pot of water to a boil and add the edamame. Cook for 4-5 minutes, or until tender.

Drain and sprinkle with sea salt.

Serve immediately.

Why it's great:
Edamame are packed with plant-based protein and fibre, making them a perfect snack for keeping you full. The sea salt enhances the flavour, making this a deliciously healthy snack option.

## 12. Guacamole with Veggie Chips

Prep Time: 5 minutes
Cook Time: 0 minutes
Servings: 1

Ingredients:

1 ripe avocado

1 tbsp lime juice

1 tbsp fresh cilantro, chopped

1/4 small onion, finely chopped

Salt and pepper to taste

1/4 cup cucumber, sliced into thin strips (for chips)

Instructions:

Scoop out the avocado flesh and mash it in a bowl.

Add lime juice, cilantro, onion, salt, and pepper, then mix until smooth.

Serve with cucumber strips as a crunchy, low-carb alternative to tortilla chips.

Why it's great:
This guacamole is rich in healthy fats from the avocado, while the cucumber provides a refreshing, crunchy alternative to chips. The combination of flavours is simple and satisfying, making it a perfect snack for any time of the day.

## 13. Cottage Cheese and Cherry Tomato Bowl

Prep Time: 5 minutes
Cook Time: 0 minutes
Servings: 1

Ingredients:

1/2 cup cottage cheese (low-fat or full-fat)

1/4 cup cherry tomatoes, halved

Salt and pepper to taste

Fresh basil or parsley for garnish (optional)

Instructions:

Spoon the cottage cheese into a bowl.

Top with halved cherry tomatoes and season with salt and pepper.

Garnish with fresh basil or parsley, if desired, and serve immediately.

Why it's great:
Cottage cheese is high in protein and pairs wonderfully with the freshness of cherry tomatoes. This simple snack is high in protein, low in carbs, and perfect for those looking for a quick, nutritious bite.

## 14. Smoked Salmon and Cream Cheese Rolls

Prep Time: 5 minutes
Cook Time: 0 minutes
Servings: 1

Ingredients:

4 slices smoked salmon

2 tbsp cream cheese

1/4 tsp fresh dill, chopped

Lemon slices for garnish

Instructions:

Spread a thin layer of cream cheese onto each slice of smoked salmon.

Sprinkle with fresh dill and roll them up.

Serve with a lemon slice on the side for a fresh, tangy kick.

Why it's great:
Smoked salmon is a fantastic source of protein and omega-3 fatty acids, while the cream cheese adds a creamy texture. This snack is quick to prepare, delicious, and full of healthy fats.

## 15. Turkey and Cheese Roll-Ups

Prep Time: 5 minutes
Cook Time: 0 minutes
Servings: 2

Ingredients:

4 slices turkey breast (deli or cooked)

2 slices cheddar cheese (or your preferred cheese)

1 tbsp mustard (optional)

Instructions:

Lay a slice of turkey flat on a surface.

Place a slice of cheese on top and roll the turkey around the cheese.

If desired, spread mustard on the inside of the turkey before rolling up.

Serve immediately.

Why it's great:
This simple snack combines lean protein from the turkey with the richness of cheese, making it both filling and low-carb. It's an easy-to-make, satisfying option for anyone craving a quick protein-packed snack.

## 16. Veggie Frittata Bites

Prep Time: 10 minutes
Cook Time: 15 minutes
Servings: 6-8 bites

Ingredients:

3 large eggs

1/4 cup spinach, chopped

1/4 cup bell peppers, chopped

1/4 cup onion, chopped

2 tbsp grated Parmesan cheese

Salt and pepper to taste

1 tbsp olive oil (for greasing)

Instructions:

Preheat the oven to 180°C (350°F) and grease a mini muffin tin with olive oil.

In a bowl, whisk the eggs and add the spinach, bell peppers, onion, Parmesan cheese, salt, and pepper.

Pour the egg mixture into the muffin tin, filling each cup about 3/4 full.

Bake for 12-15 minutes, or until the frittata bites are set and lightly golden.

Serve immediately or store for later.

Why it's great:
These veggie-packed frittata bites are a high-protein, low-carb snack that you can make ahead. The eggs provide a great source of protein, while the vegetables add fibre and essential vitamins.

## 17. Cucumber and Hummus Bites

Prep Time: 5 minutes
Cook Time: 0 minutes
Servings: 1

Ingredients:

1 cucumber, sliced

3 tbsp hummus

Instructions:

Slice the cucumber into rounds.

Top each cucumber slice with a spoonful of hummus.

Serve immediately.

Why it's great:
This is a light and refreshing snack, packed with protein and fibre. The cucumber provides a crunchy, hydrating base, while the hummus adds healthy fats and protein, making this a simple and delicious low-carb snack.

## 18. Almond Butter Celery Sticks

Prep Time: 5 minutes
Cook Time: 0 minutes
Servings: 1

Ingredients:

2 celery stalks, cut into sticks

2 tbsp almond butter

Instructions:

Slice the celery into sticks.

Spread almond butter on each celery stick.

Serve immediately.

Why it's great:
This is a simple, satisfying snack combining the fibre-rich celery with the protein and healthy fats from almond butter. It's a great way to curb hunger and provide a burst of energy without carbs.

## 19. Mini Cucumber and Cheese Bites

Prep Time: 5 minutes
Cook Time: 0 minutes
Servings: 2

Ingredients:

1 cucumber, sliced into rounds

1/4 cup cream cheese or goat cheese

Fresh dill for garnish (optional)

Salt and pepper to taste

Instructions:

Slice the cucumber into rounds and place them on a serving plate.

Spread a thin layer of cream cheese or goat cheese on each cucumber slice.

Season with salt and pepper, and garnish with fresh dill, if desired.

Serve immediately.

Why it's great:
This snack is light yet filling, combining the hydrating crunch of cucumber with the creamy richness of cheese. It's an excellent source of protein and healthy fats, making it a perfect low-carb option.

## 20. Turkey Avocado Roll-Ups

Prep Time: 5 minutes
Cook Time: 0 minutes
Servings: 1

Ingredients:

3 slices turkey breast

1/2 avocado, sliced

1 tbsp mustard or mayo (optional)

Instructions:

Lay the slices of turkey flat on a plate.

Place a slice of avocado on each turkey slice and roll them up tightly.

If desired, spread mustard or mayo on the turkey before rolling it up.

Serve immediately.

Why it's great:
This snack combines lean turkey with healthy fats from avocado, making it a satisfying and filling snack. It's high in protein and low in carbs, perfect for keeping your energy levels steady throughout the day.

Conclusion
These high-protein, low-carb snacks are designed to keep you satisfied, fuel your body, and help you stick to your healthy eating goals. From quick and easy options like hard-boiled eggs and cheese-stuffed olives to more creative recipes like veggie frittata bites, you'll find plenty of delicious and nutritious snacks to enjoy between meals.

# Chapter 6: Desserts

## Overview of Low-Carb, High-Protein Desserts

Desserts don't have to be off-limits when following a low-carb, high-protein diet. In fact, you can still enjoy sweet treats without derailing your health goals. The key is to swap out traditional high-carb ingredients with low-carb alternatives and focus on high-protein options that satisfy your sweet tooth while providing essential nutrients.

This chapter will guide you through 20 guilt-free, high-protein dessert recipes that are both delicious and nutritious. From rich chocolate mousse to fruity chia puddings, these desserts are made with wholesome ingredients that will support your fitness and health journey without compromising on taste.

## 1. Coconut Macaroons

Prep Time: 10 minutes
Cook Time: 15 minutes
Servings: 12 macaroons

Ingredients:

1 1/2 cups unsweetened shredded coconut

1/4 cup almond flour

2 large egg whites

1 tbsp vanilla extract

1-2 tbsp stevia or preferred sweetener

1/4 tsp salt

Instructions:

Preheat the oven to 175°C (350°F) and line a baking sheet with parchment paper.

In a bowl, combine the shredded coconut, almond flour, egg whites, vanilla extract, sweetener, and salt.

Mix until well combined and form into small mounds on the baking sheet.

Bake for 12-15 minutes, or until golden brown.

Allow to cool before serving.

Why it's great:
These coconut macaroons are naturally low in carbs and rich in healthy fats from coconut, making them a perfect dessert that provides a protein boost and a satisfying sweet treat.

## 2. Chocolate Protein Balls

Prep Time: 5 minutes
Cook Time: 0 minutes
Servings: 12 balls

Ingredients:

1 scoop chocolate protein powder

1/4 cup almond butter

2 tbsp cocoa powder

1 tbsp honey or stevia

1/4 cup unsweetened shredded coconut

1-2 tbsp water (if needed)

Instructions:

In a bowl, combine the protein powder, almond butter, cocoa powder, honey, and shredded coconut.

Mix well until the mixture becomes firm and dough-like. Add water if necessary to reach the desired consistency.

Roll the mixture into 12 small balls.

Store in the fridge for 30 minutes to firm up before serving.

Why it's great:
These chocolate protein balls are packed with protein and healthy fats. They're a quick and easy way to satisfy a chocolate craving while staying on track with your low-carb, high-protein goals.

## 3. Sugar-Free Almond Flour Cookies

Prep Time: 10 minutes
Cook Time: 12 minutes
Servings: 12 cookies

Ingredients:

1 1/2 cups almond flour

1/4 cup erythritol or sweetener of choice

1 large egg

1/4 cup butter, melted

1 tsp vanilla extract

1/4 tsp baking soda

1/4 tsp salt

Instructions:

Preheat the oven to 175°C (350°F) and line a baking sheet with parchment paper.

In a bowl, mix the almond flour, sweetener, baking soda, and salt.

Add the egg, melted butter, and vanilla extract and mix until combined.

Scoop spoonfuls of the dough onto the baking sheet and flatten slightly.

Bake for 10-12 minutes until golden brown around the edges.

Allow to cool before serving.

Why it's great:
These almond flour cookies are sugar-free and gluten-free, making them a great option for those following a low-carb, high-protein diet. Almond flour is a low-carb, high-protein alternative to traditional flour, giving these cookies a satisfying texture.

## 4. Avocado Chocolate Mousse

Prep Time: 5 minutes
Cook Time: 0 minutes
Servings: 2

Ingredients:

1 ripe avocado

2 tbsp cocoa powder

2 tbsp stevia or sweetener of choice

1 tsp vanilla extract

2 tbsp unsweetened almond milk

Instructions:

Scoop the avocado flesh into a blender or food processor.

Add the cocoa powder, sweetener, vanilla extract, and almond milk.

Blend until smooth and creamy.

Refrigerate for 30 minutes before serving for a chilled mousse.

Why it's great:
This avocado chocolate mousse is rich and creamy, made with healthy fats from avocado. It's naturally low in carbs and provides a good dose of protein, while satisfying your chocolate cravings.

## 5. Low-Carb Cheesecake Bites

Prep Time: 10 minutes
Cook Time: 10 minutes
Servings: 12 bites

Ingredients:

1 cup cream cheese, softened

1/2 cup Greek yogurt (unsweetened)

1/4 cup stevia or sweetener of choice

1/2 tsp vanilla extract

1/4 cup almond flour (for crust)

1 tbsp butter, melted (for crust)

1 tbsp coconut flour (for crust)

Instructions:

Preheat the oven to 175°C (350°F) and line a muffin tin with paper liners.

In a bowl, combine the almond flour, coconut flour, and melted butter. Press the mixture into the bottom of each muffin liner to form the crust.

In a separate bowl, mix the cream cheese, Greek yogurt, stevia, and vanilla extract until smooth.

Spoon the cream cheese mixture over the crusts in the muffin tin.

Bake for 10 minutes, then refrigerate for 1-2 hours before serving.

Why it's great:
These cheesecake bites are a low-carb twist on traditional cheesecake, using cream cheese and Greek yogurt for a high-protein base. The almond flour crust adds healthy fats without the carbs, making these bites a delicious, guilt-free dessert.

## 6. Peanut Butter Protein Bars

Prep Time: 10 minutes
Cook Time: 20 minutes
Servings: 8 bars

Ingredients:

1 cup peanut butter (unsweetened)

1 scoop vanilla protein powder

1/4 cup almond flour

2 tbsp honey or stevia

1/4 cup almond milk

Instructions:

Preheat the oven to 180°C (350°F) and grease a baking dish.

In a bowl, mix the peanut butter, protein powder, almond flour, honey, and almond milk until smooth.

Pour the mixture into the prepared baking dish and press it down evenly.

Bake for 18-20 minutes or until firm and golden on top.

Allow to cool before cutting into bars.

Why it's great:
These peanut butter protein bars are a great source of protein and healthy fats, providing a satisfying and energizing snack or dessert. They're low in carbs and perfect for a post-workout treat.

## 7. Berry Chia Pudding

Prep Time: 5 minutes
Cook Time: 0 minutes (requires overnight refrigeration)
Servings: 1

Ingredients:

2 tbsp chia seeds

1/2 cup unsweetened almond milk

1/4 cup mixed berries

1 tsp stevia or honey (optional)

Instructions:

In a jar, combine the chia seeds and almond milk. Stir well to combine.

Refrigerate overnight to allow the chia seeds to absorb the liquid and thicken.

Top with mixed berries and sweetener if desired.

Serve chilled.

Why it's great:
Chia pudding is a great high-protein, low-carb dessert or snack. Chia seeds are full of fibre and omega-3s, and this pudding is a perfect make-ahead option for busy days.

## 8. Keto-Friendly Chocolate Cupcakes

Prep Time: 10 minutes
Cook Time: 15 minutes
Servings: 6 cupcakes

Ingredients:

1/2 cup almond flour

2 tbsp cocoa powder

1/4 cup stevia or sweetener of choice

1/2 tsp baking powder

2 large eggs

1/4 cup unsweetened almond milk

1/4 cup melted coconut oil

1 tsp vanilla extract

Instructions:

Preheat the oven to 180°C (350°F) and line a muffin tin with paper liners.

In a bowl, mix the almond flour, cocoa powder, stevia, and baking powder.

In a separate bowl, whisk the eggs, almond milk, melted coconut oil, and vanilla extract.

Combine the wet and dry ingredients, then divide the batter evenly into the muffin tin.

Bake for 12-15 minutes, or until a toothpick comes out clean.

Let cool before serving.

Why it's great:
These keto-friendly chocolate cupcakes are low in carbs and rich in healthy fats from coconut oil. They provide a delicious way to satisfy your chocolate cravings while keeping your carbs in check.

## 9. Almond Flour Cake with Cream Cheese Frosting

Prep Time: 15 minutes
Cook Time: 30 minutes
Servings: 8

Ingredients:

1 1/2 cups almond flour

1/4 cup stevia or sweetener of choice

1/4 tsp baking powder

2 large eggs

1/4 cup unsweetened almond milk

1/4 cup melted butter

1/2 cup cream cheese, softened

2 tbsp powdered sweetener

1/2 tsp vanilla extract

Instructions:

Preheat the oven to 180°C (350°F) and grease a cake pan.

In a bowl, mix the almond flour, stevia, and baking powder.

In another bowl, whisk the eggs, almond milk, and melted butter.

Combine the wet and dry ingredients, then pour the batter into the cake pan.

Bake for 25-30 minutes, or until a toothpick comes out clean.

While the cake is cooling, beat the cream cheese, powdered sweetener, and vanilla extract until smooth.

Frost the cooled cake with the cream cheese frosting and serve.

Why it's great:
This almond flour cake is low in carbs and gluten-free, while the cream cheese frosting adds a rich, satisfying touch. It's a great dessert option for those following a low-carb, high-protein diet.

## 10. Baked Apple Cinnamon Protein Bars

Prep Time: 10 minutes
Cook Time: 20 minutes
Servings: 12 bars

Ingredients:

1 cup almond flour

1 scoop vanilla protein powder

1/2 tsp cinnamon

1/4 tsp nutmeg

1/4 tsp baking powder

1/4 cup unsweetened applesauce

2 large eggs

1/4 cup stevia or sweetener of choice

1 tsp vanilla extract

Instructions:

Preheat the oven to 175°C (350°F) and line a baking pan with parchment paper.

In a bowl, mix the almond flour, protein powder, cinnamon, nutmeg, and baking powder.

In a separate bowl, whisk the applesauce, eggs, stevia, and vanilla extract.

Combine the wet and dry ingredients and pour the batter into the prepared pan.

Bake for 18-20 minutes, or until a toothpick comes out clean.

Allow the bars to cool before cutting into squares.

Why it's great:
These protein bars are perfect for those craving something sweet with a touch of spice. They are low-carb, protein-packed, and full of natural sweetness from the applesauce. They also make for a great grab-and-go snack.

## 11. Chia Seed Chocolate Pudding

Prep Time: 5 minutes
Cook Time: 0 minutes (requires overnight refrigeration)
Servings: 2

Ingredients:

2 tbsp chia seeds

1 cup unsweetened almond milk

1 tbsp cocoa powder

1-2 tbsp stevia or sweetener of choice

1/2 tsp vanilla extract

Instructions:

In a bowl, combine the chia seeds, almond milk, cocoa powder, sweetener, and vanilla extract.

Stir well to ensure the cocoa powder is fully dissolved and the chia seeds are evenly distributed.

Cover and refrigerate overnight to allow the pudding to thicken.

Stir the pudding before serving and enjoy.

Why it's great:
Chia seeds are packed with fibre and healthy fats, while cocoa powder provides a rich chocolate flavour. This pudding is an easy, no-cook dessert that's both low in carbs and high in protein.

## 12. Low-Carb Pumpkin Pie Bites

Prep Time: 10 minutes
Cook Time: 15 minutes
Servings: 12 bites

Ingredients:

1 cup canned pumpkin puree

1/2 cup almond flour

1 scoop vanilla protein powder

1/4 tsp cinnamon

1/4 tsp nutmeg

2 tbsp stevia or sweetener of choice

1 large egg

1/4 tsp baking powder

Instructions:

Preheat the oven to 175°C (350°F) and grease a mini muffin tin.

In a bowl, combine the pumpkin puree, almond flour, protein powder, cinnamon, nutmeg, sweetener, egg, and baking powder.

Mix until smooth, then spoon the mixture into the muffin tin.

Bake for 12-15 minutes, or until the bites are firm and a toothpick comes out clean.

Allow to cool before serving.

Why it's great:
These pumpkin pie bites are a delicious fall-inspired dessert with all the flavours of pumpkin pie but without the carbs. The protein powder and almond flour help keep this dessert low-carb and satisfying.

## 13. Chocolate-Covered Almonds

Prep Time: 5 minutes
Cook Time: 10 minutes
Servings: 1

Ingredients:

1/4 cup dark chocolate (85% cocoa or higher)

1/4 cup almonds, raw or roasted

1 tbsp coconut oil

Instructions:

In a small pan, melt the dark chocolate with coconut oil over low heat, stirring constantly.

Once melted, dip each almond into the chocolate and place them on a parchment-lined tray.

Refrigerate for 10-15 minutes to allow the chocolate to harden.

Serve immediately or store in the fridge for later.

Why it's great:
These chocolate-covered almonds provide a satisfying crunch and protein from the almonds, while the dark chocolate offers rich flavour with minimal sugar. They're a perfect treat to satisfy your sweet cravings.

## 14. Keto Peanut Butter Cups

Prep Time: 10 minutes
Cook Time: 5 minutes
Servings: 6

Ingredients:

1/4 cup peanut butter (unsweetened)

2 tbsp coconut oil

1/4 cup dark chocolate (85% cocoa or higher)

2 tbsp stevia or sweetener of choice

1/4 tsp vanilla extract

Instructions:

Melt the peanut butter and coconut oil together in a small pan over low heat.

Once melted, stir in the stevia and vanilla extract.

In a separate pan, melt the dark chocolate until smooth.

Line a muffin tin with paper liners, then pour a layer of chocolate into the bottom of each liner.

Add a spoonful of the peanut butter mixture on top, followed by another layer of melted chocolate.

Refrigerate for 20 minutes to set, then serve.

Why it's great:
These keto peanut butter cups are low in carbs and rich in protein and healthy fats. They're a delicious treat that satisfies your sweet cravings without spiking your blood sugar levels.

## 15. Lemon Protein Bars

Prep Time: 10 minutes
Cook Time: 25 minutes
Servings: 8 bars

Ingredients:

1 1/2 cups almond flour

1 scoop vanilla protein powder

1/4 cup stevia or sweetener of choice

1/4 tsp baking powder

1/4 tsp salt

2 large eggs

1/4 cup lemon juice

1 tbsp lemon zest

1/4 cup unsweetened almond milk

Instructions:

Preheat the oven to 180°C (350°F) and grease a baking pan.

In a bowl, mix the almond flour, protein powder, sweetener, baking powder, and salt.

In a separate bowl, whisk the eggs, lemon juice, lemon zest, and almond milk.

Combine the wet and dry ingredients, then pour the batter into the prepared pan.

Bake for 20-25 minutes, or until the bars are set and a toothpick comes out clean.

Allow to cool before cutting into bars and serving.

Why it's great:
These lemon protein bars are fresh and tangy, with the perfect balance of protein and healthy fats. They're a refreshing dessert or snack that's low in carbs and full of flavour.

## 16. Chocolate-Dipped Strawberries

Prep Time: 5 minutes
Cook Time: 10 minutes
Servings: 4

Ingredients:

1/2 cup dark chocolate (85% cocoa or higher)

8 large strawberries

1 tbsp coconut oil

Instructions:

Melt the dark chocolate and coconut oil together in a small saucepan over low heat, stirring constantly.

Dip each strawberry into the melted chocolate, coating it halfway.

Place the dipped strawberries on a parchment-lined tray and refrigerate for 10-15 minutes to set the chocolate.

Serve immediately or store in the fridge.

Why it's great:
Chocolate-dipped strawberries are a classic, low-carb treat. The strawberries are rich in antioxidants, and the dark chocolate provides a satisfying, healthy sweet treat without excess sugar.

## 17. No-Bake Protein Cheesecake Bites

Prep Time: 10 minutes
Cook Time: 0 minutes (requires refrigeration)
Servings: 10-12 bites

Ingredients:

1 cup cream cheese, softened

1/2 cup Greek yogurt (unsweetened)

1 scoop vanilla protein powder

2 tbsp stevia or sweetener of choice

1 tsp vanilla extract

1/4 cup almond flour (for the base)

1 tbsp coconut oil, melted (for the base)

Instructions:

In a bowl, mix together the cream cheese, Greek yogurt, protein powder, stevia, and vanilla extract until smooth.

In a separate bowl, combine the almond flour and melted coconut oil. Press this mixture into the bottom of silicone molds or mini muffin tins to form the crust.

Spoon the cheesecake mixture over the almond flour crust and smooth the top.

Refrigerate for 2-3 hours to set before serving.

Why it's great:
These no-bake cheesecake bites are creamy, rich, and full of protein. The combination of Greek yogurt and protein powder makes them a satisfying dessert with minimal carbs, while the almond flour crust adds a nice texture.

## 18. Keto Chocolate Pudding

Prep Time: 5 minutes
Cook Time: 5 minutes
Servings: 2

Ingredients:

1 cup unsweetened almond milk

2 tbsp cocoa powder

2 tbsp stevia or sweetener of choice

1/2 tsp vanilla extract

1/2 cup heavy cream

1 tbsp chia seeds (optional for thickening)

Instructions:

In a saucepan, heat the almond milk over medium heat until warm.

Whisk in the cocoa powder, sweetener, vanilla extract, and chia seeds (if using).

Stir in the heavy cream and cook for 3-5 minutes until the mixture thickens to a pudding-like consistency.

Pour into serving bowls and refrigerate for 1 hour before serving.

Why it's great:
This keto chocolate pudding is rich and creamy, satisfying your chocolate cravings without the sugar. The heavy cream adds a luscious texture, while the cocoa powder provides a deep chocolate flavour.

## 19. Low-Carb Raspberry Sorbet

Prep Time: 5 minutes
Cook Time: 0 minutes (requires freezing)
Servings: 2

Ingredients:

1 cup raspberries (fresh or frozen)

1 tbsp stevia or sweetener of choice

1/4 cup unsweetened almond milk

1 tbsp lemon juice

Instructions:

In a blender or food processor, combine the raspberries, sweetener, almond milk, and lemon juice.

Blend until smooth, then pour the mixture into a shallow dish.

Freeze for 3-4 hours, stirring occasionally to prevent ice crystals from forming.

Serve immediately or store in the freezer for later.

Why it's great:
This raspberry sorbet is a refreshing, low-carb dessert made with fresh fruit. It's naturally sweetened and perfect for cooling off during warmer months. The almond milk gives it a creamy texture, while the raspberries provide antioxidants and flavour.

## 20. Keto Lemon Bars

Prep Time: 10 minutes
Cook Time: 25 minutes
Servings: 8 bars

Ingredients:

Crust:

1 1/2 cups almond flour

1/4 cup melted butter

2 tbsp stevia or sweetener of choice

1/4 tsp salt

Filling:

1/2 cup fresh lemon juice

2 large eggs

1/4 cup stevia or sweetener of choice

1/4 cup almond flour

1/4 tsp vanilla extract

Instructions:

Preheat the oven to 180°C (350°F) and grease a baking dish.

In a bowl, mix the almond flour, melted butter, sweetener, and salt for the crust.

Press the mixture into the bottom of the baking dish and bake for 10-12 minutes, until lightly golden.

In a separate bowl, whisk together the lemon juice, eggs, sweetener, almond flour, and vanilla extract for the filling.

Pour the filling over the baked crust and return the dish to the oven for another 12-15 minutes, or until the filling is set.

Allow to cool before cutting into squares and serving.

Why it's great:
These keto lemon bars offer the perfect balance of tangy lemon and sweetness while being low in carbs. The almond flour crust adds a rich, nutty texture, while the lemon filling provides a refreshing contrast. This is a great option for anyone craving a citrusy dessert without the sugar.

## 21. Keto Chocolate Chip Cookies

Prep Time: 10 minutes
Cook Time: 12 minutes
Servings: 12 cookies

Ingredients:

1 cup almond flour

1/2 cup stevia or sweetener of choice

1/4 tsp baking soda

1/4 tsp salt

1/4 cup butter, melted

1 large egg

1 tsp vanilla extract

1/4 cup sugar-free chocolate chips

Instructions:

Preheat the oven to 180°C (350°F) and line a baking sheet with parchment paper.

In a bowl, combine the almond flour, sweetener, baking soda, and salt.

Add the melted butter, egg, and vanilla extract to the dry ingredients, mixing until smooth.

Stir in the sugar-free chocolate chips.

Scoop spoonfuls of the dough onto the baking sheet, flattening them slightly.

Bake for 10-12 minutes, or until the cookies are golden around the edges.

Let cool before serving.

Why it's great:
These keto chocolate chip cookies provide all the classic cookie flavour but without the carbs. They're soft, chewy, and full of rich chocolate flavour, making them a perfect low-carb dessert or snack.

## 22. Keto Strawberry Cheesecake

Prep Time: 10 minutes
Cook Time: 25 minutes
Servings: 6

Ingredients:

Crust:

1 cup almond flour

1/4 cup melted butter

1 tbsp stevia or sweetener of choice

Filling:

2 cups cream cheese, softened

1/2 cup Greek yogurt (unsweetened)

1/4 cup stevia or sweetener of choice

1 tsp vanilla extract

1/4 cup fresh strawberries, chopped

Instructions:

Preheat the oven to 180°C (350°F) and grease a small cheesecake pan.

For the crust, mix the almond flour, melted butter, and sweetener in a bowl. Press the mixture into the bottom of the cheesecake pan.

Bake for 8-10 minutes, or until lightly golden.

For the filling, beat the cream cheese, Greek yogurt, sweetener, and vanilla extract until smooth.

Gently fold in the chopped strawberries.

Pour the filling over the baked crust and bake for 20-25 minutes, or until the cheesecake is set.

Let the cheesecake cool in the fridge for a few hours before serving.

Why it's great:
This keto strawberry cheesecake offers a rich, creamy texture with a fresh strawberry twist. The almond flour crust is low in carbs, while the filling is high in protein and healthy fats, making it a satisfying and indulgent dessert.

# Chapter 7: Drinks

**Overview of Low-Carb, High-Protein Drinks**

When following a low-carb, high-protein diet, your drinks should not only complement your nutritional goals but also provide a delicious way to fuel your body with essential nutrients. Protein-packed beverages are an excellent option to help you stay energized, curb hunger, and support muscle recovery—whether you need a refreshing smoothie, an energizing coffee, or a soothing tea.

This chapter includes 20 delicious, high-protein, low-carb drinks that can be enjoyed throughout the day. These drinks are designed to boost your protein intake, enhance your metabolism, and satisfy your thirst while keeping carbs to a minimum. Whether you're looking for a post-workout shake, a mid-afternoon energy boost, or a relaxing evening beverage, you'll find the perfect options here.

## 1. Protein Smoothie with Almond Butter

Prep Time: 5 minutes
Cook Time: 0 minutes
Servings: 1

Ingredients:

1 scoop vanilla protein powder

1 tbsp almond butter

1/2 cup unsweetened almond milk

1/2 banana

1/4 tsp cinnamon

1/2 cup ice cubes

Instructions:

Add the protein powder, almond butter, almond milk, banana, and cinnamon to a blender.

Blend until smooth and creamy, adding more almond milk if needed for desired consistency.

Add ice cubes and blend again until chilled.

Serve immediately.

Why it's great:
This smoothie is rich in protein from the powder and almond butter, with healthy fats from the almond butter that help keep you full. The banana adds natural sweetness and creaminess, while cinnamon offers a warm flavour boost.

## 2. Green Protein Smoothie

Prep Time: 5 minutes
Cook Time: 0 minutes
Servings: 1

Ingredients:

1 scoop plant-based protein powder

1 cup spinach

1/4 avocado

1/2 cup unsweetened almond milk

1 tbsp chia seeds

1/2 lemon, juiced

1/2 cup ice cubes

Instructions:

Add the protein powder, spinach, avocado, almond milk, chia seeds, lemon juice, and ice cubes to a blender.

Blend until smooth and creamy.

Serve immediately.

Why it's great:
Packed with plant-based protein and healthy fats from avocado, this smoothie is rich in nutrients and provides an energy boost. Spinach adds fibre and vitamins, making this an ideal way to start the day or recover after a workout.

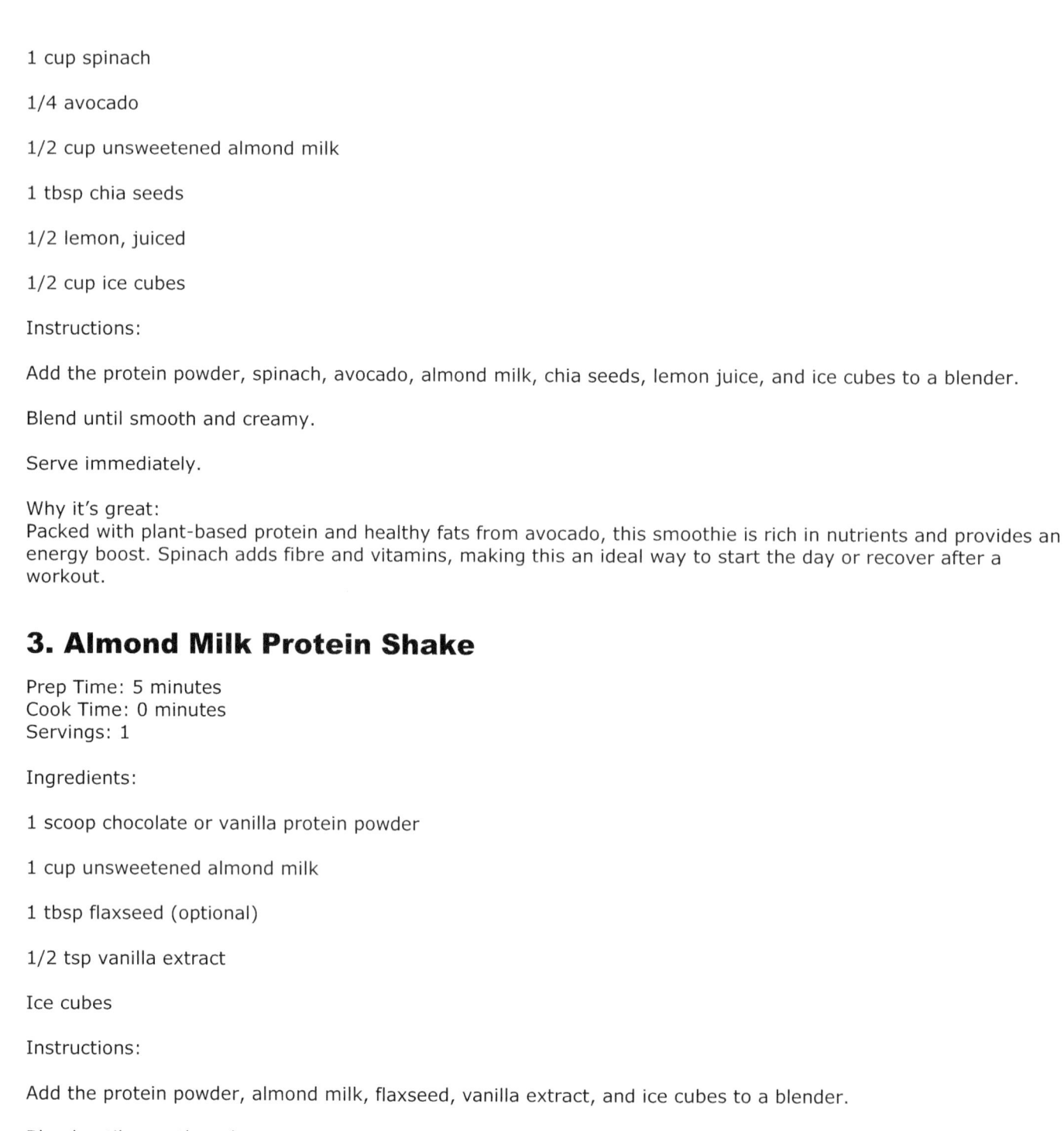

## 3. Almond Milk Protein Shake

Prep Time: 5 minutes
Cook Time: 0 minutes
Servings: 1

Ingredients:

1 scoop chocolate or vanilla protein powder

1 cup unsweetened almond milk

1 tbsp flaxseed (optional)

1/2 tsp vanilla extract

Ice cubes

Instructions:

Add the protein powder, almond milk, flaxseed, vanilla extract, and ice cubes to a blender.

Blend until smooth and creamy.

Serve immediately.

Why it's great:
Almond milk is low in carbs and adds a smooth, nutty flavour to this protein shake. The flaxseed provides extra fibre and omega-3 fatty acids, making this shake an excellent, nutrient-dense drink.

## 4. Collagen-Infused Lemonade

Prep Time: 5 minutes
Cook Time: 0 minutes
Servings: 1

Ingredients:

1 scoop unflavoured collagen powder

1 cup water

1/2 lemon, juiced

1-2 tsp stevia or sweetener of choice

Ice cubes

Instructions:

Mix the collagen powder, water, lemon juice, and sweetener in a glass.

Stir until the collagen powder dissolves completely.

Add ice cubes and serve chilled.

Why it's great:
Collagen is excellent for skin, hair, and joint health, and this lemonade is a refreshing, hydrating way to enjoy its benefits. The lemon adds a burst of vitamin C, while stevia keeps the sugar content low.

## 5. Chocolate Almond Protein Shake

Prep Time: 5 minutes
Cook Time: 0 minutes
Servings: 1

Ingredients:

1 scoop chocolate protein powder

1 cup unsweetened almond milk

1 tbsp almond butter

1 tbsp unsweetened cocoa powder

1 tsp vanilla extract

Ice cubes

Instructions:

Add the chocolate protein powder, almond milk, almond butter, cocoa powder, vanilla extract, and ice cubes to a blender.

Blend until smooth and creamy.

Serve immediately.

Why it's great:
This protein shake is indulgent and rich in flavour, with healthy fats from almond butter and a protein boost from the powder. The unsweetened cocoa powder gives it a rich, chocolatey taste without added sugars.

## 6. Coconut Water Protein Drink

Prep Time: 5 minutes
Cook Time: 0 minutes
Servings: 1

Ingredients:

1 scoop coconut-flavored protein powder

1 cup coconut water

1 tbsp chia seeds (optional)

1/4 cup pineapple, diced (optional for sweetness)

Instructions:

Add the protein powder, coconut water, chia seeds, and pineapple (if using) to a blender.

Blend until smooth and creamy.

Serve immediately.

Why it's great:
Coconut water is hydrating and rich in electrolytes, making it perfect for post-workout recovery. This protein drink combines the benefits of coconut water with a healthy protein boost, making it both refreshing and nourishing.

## 7. Matcha Protein Latte

Prep Time: 5 minutes
Cook Time: 5 minutes
Servings: 1

Ingredients:

1 scoop vanilla protein powder

1 tsp matcha green tea powder

1 cup unsweetened almond milk

1 tsp stevia or sweetener of choice

1/4 tsp vanilla extract

Ice cubes (optional for iced latte)

Instructions:

Heat the almond milk in a small saucepan until warm.

Whisk the matcha powder into the warm almond milk until fully dissolved.

Add the protein powder, stevia, and vanilla extract, stirring until smooth.

If making an iced latte, add ice cubes to a glass and pour the mixture over.

Serve immediately.

Why it's great:
This matcha latte provides a smooth, creamy beverage with a caffeine boost from matcha. The protein powder adds a satisfying richness, while the almond milk and stevia keep the drink low in carbs.

## 8. Iced Coffee Protein Shake

Prep Time: 5 minutes
Cook Time: 0 minutes
Servings: 1

Ingredients:

1 scoop vanilla or chocolate protein powder

1 cup cold brewed coffee

1/2 cup unsweetened almond milk

1 tbsp stevia or sweetener of choice

Ice cubes

Instructions:

Add the protein powder, cold brewed coffee, almond milk, and sweetener to a blender.

Add ice cubes and blend until smooth and chilled.

Serve immediately.

Why it's great:
This iced coffee protein shake combines the energizing effects of coffee with a protein-packed boost, making it the perfect drink for an afternoon pick-me-up. The almond milk keeps it creamy, while the stevia adds sweetness without the carbs.

## 9. Green Tea with Ginger and Lemon

Prep Time: 5 minutes
Cook Time: 5 minutes
Servings: 1

Ingredients:

1 green tea bag

1/2 tsp fresh ginger, grated

1/2 lemon, juiced

Stevia or honey to taste

Instructions:

Brew the green tea bag in hot water for 3-5 minutes.

Stir in the grated ginger and lemon juice.

Sweeten with stevia or honey, if desired, and serve warm.

Why it's great:
Green tea is packed with antioxidants, while ginger aids in digestion and provides a warming, aromatic flavour. The lemon adds a refreshing twist, making this a soothing, healthy beverage.

## 10. Low-Carb Chocolate Milkshake

Prep Time: 5 minutes
Cook Time: 0 minutes
Servings: 1

Ingredients:

1 scoop chocolate protein powder

1 cup unsweetened almond milk

1 tbsp almond butter

1/2 tsp vanilla extract

Ice cubes

Instructions:

Add the chocolate protein powder, almond milk, almond butter, and vanilla extract to a blender.

Add ice cubes and blend until smooth and creamy.

Serve immediately.

Why it's great:
This chocolate milkshake is rich and indulgent but still low in carbs. The protein powder and almond butter provide a filling and nutritious base, while the ice gives it a frosty texture.

## 11. Coconut Protein Smoothie

Prep Time: 5 minutes
Cook Time: 0 minutes
Servings: 1

Ingredients:

1 scoop coconut-flavored protein powder

1/2 cup coconut milk (unsweetened)

1/2 cup unsweetened almond milk

1 tbsp shredded coconut (unsweetened)

1/2 cup ice cubes

1 tbsp stevia or sweetener of choice

Instructions:

Add the protein powder, coconut milk, almond milk, shredded coconut, and stevia to a blender.

Blend until smooth and creamy.

Add ice cubes and blend again until chilled.

Serve immediately.

Why it's great:
Coconut is a great source of healthy fats, and this smoothie provides a refreshing tropical taste while also packing in protein. The combination of coconut milk and shredded coconut enhances the flavour and texture, making it both delicious and filling.

## 12. Protein-Packed Mocha Shake

Prep Time: 5 minutes
Cook Time: 0 minutes
Servings: 1

Ingredients:

1 scoop chocolate protein powder

1/2 cup brewed coffee, cooled

1/2 cup unsweetened almond milk

1 tbsp cocoa powder

1 tbsp stevia or sweetener of choice

Ice cubes

Instructions:

In a blender, combine the chocolate protein powder, cooled coffee, almond milk, cocoa powder, and stevia.

Blend until smooth and well-combined.

Add ice cubes and blend again until chilled.

Serve immediately.

Why it's great:
This mocha shake offers the perfect combination of caffeine from the coffee and protein from the shake, making it a great option for a morning boost or afternoon pick-me-up. The chocolate and coffee blend together for a rich, indulgent flavour without the carbs.

## 13. Cucumber Mint Protein Smoothie

Prep Time: 5 minutes
Cook Time: 0 minutes
Servings: 1

Ingredients:

1 scoop vanilla protein powder

1/2 cucumber, chopped

1/4 cup fresh mint leaves

1/2 cup unsweetened almond milk

1 tbsp lime juice

1 tbsp stevia or sweetener of choice

Ice cubes

Instructions:

Add the protein powder, cucumber, mint leaves, almond milk, lime juice, and stevia to a blender.

Blend until smooth and creamy.

Add ice cubes and blend again until chilled.

Serve immediately.

Why it's great:
This smoothie is refreshing and hydrating, thanks to the cucumber and mint. The lime juice adds a citrusy tang, and the protein powder makes it a filling snack or meal replacement. It's perfect for those warm days when you want something light yet satisfying.

## 14. Protein-Rich Fruit Smoothie

Prep Time: 5 minutes
Cook Time: 0 minutes
Servings: 1

Ingredients:

1 scoop vanilla or berry-flavored protein powder

1/2 cup strawberries

1/4 cup blueberries

1/2 cup unsweetened almond milk

1/2 tbsp chia seeds

Ice cubes

Instructions:

Add the protein powder, strawberries, blueberries, almond milk, and chia seeds to a blender.

Blend until smooth and creamy.

Add ice cubes and blend again until chilled.

Serve immediately.

Why it's great:
This smoothie is packed with antioxidants from the berries and omega-3s from the chia seeds. The protein powder provides the necessary protein boost, making this a satisfying and nutrient-dense drink.

## 15. Iced Matcha Protein Latte

Prep Time: 5 minutes
Cook Time: 0 minutes
Servings: 1

Ingredients:

1 scoop vanilla protein powder

1 tsp matcha powder

1/2 cup unsweetened almond milk

1/2 cup cold water

1 tbsp stevia or sweetener of choice

Ice cubes

Instructions:

Whisk the matcha powder with the cold water until it is fully dissolved.

Add the protein powder, almond milk, and stevia to the matcha mixture.

Stir or blend until smooth and well-combined.

Add ice cubes and stir again.

Serve immediately.

Why it's great:
This iced matcha latte is energizing and packed with antioxidants. Matcha provides a slow-releasing caffeine boost, while the protein powder ensures you're getting a high-protein drink to keep you satisfied throughout the day.

## 16. Protein-Packed Coconut Smoothie

Prep Time: 5 minutes
Cook Time: 0 minutes
Servings: 1

Ingredients:

1 scoop vanilla protein powder

1/2 cup unsweetened coconut milk

1/4 cup unsweetened shredded coconut

1/2 cup pineapple, diced

1 tbsp stevia or sweetener of choice

Ice cubes

Instructions:

Add the protein powder, coconut milk, shredded coconut, pineapple, and stevia to a blender.

Blend until smooth and creamy.

Add ice cubes and blend again until chilled.

Serve immediately.

Why it's great:
This smoothie is rich in protein and healthy fats from coconut milk and shredded coconut, with a sweet tropical flavour from the pineapple. It's a satisfying and hydrating drink, perfect for a quick snack or post-workout treat.

## 17. Mocha Protein Latte

Prep Time: 5 minutes
Cook Time: 5 minutes
Servings: 1

**Ingredients:**

1 scoop chocolate protein powder

1/2 cup brewed coffee, cooled

1/2 cup unsweetened almond milk

1 tbsp cocoa powder

1 tsp vanilla extract

Ice cubes

**Instructions:**

Brew the coffee and let it cool.

In a blender, combine the cooled coffee, protein powder, almond milk, cocoa powder, and vanilla extract.

Blend until smooth and creamy.

Add ice cubes and blend again until chilled.

Serve immediately.

**Why it's great:**
This mocha protein latte combines the energizing effects of coffee with a protein boost from the protein powder. It's a rich, indulgent drink that keeps you fueled and satisfied while being low in carbs.

## 18. Protein-Packed Green Juice

Prep Time: 5 minutes
Cook Time: 0 minutes
Servings: 1

**Ingredients:**

1 scoop plant-based protein powder

1/2 cup spinach

1/2 cucumber, sliced

1/4 green apple, sliced

1/2 lemon, juiced

1 cup cold water

Ice cubes

**Instructions:**

Add the protein powder, spinach, cucumber, green apple, lemon juice, and cold water to a blender.

Blend until smooth and creamy.

Add ice cubes and blend again until chilled.

Serve immediately.

**Why it's great:**
This green juice is loaded with vegetables and fruit, providing a healthy dose of vitamins and minerals. The protein powder ensures you're getting a filling, nutrient-packed drink that helps support muscle growth and recovery.

## 19. Strawberry Protein Smoothie

Prep Time: 5 minutes
Cook Time: 0 minutes
Servings: 1

**Ingredients:**

1 scoop vanilla protein powder

1/2 cup strawberries

1/2 cup unsweetened almond milk

1 tbsp flaxseed

Ice cubes

### Instructions:

Add the protein powder, strawberries, almond milk, and flaxseed to a blender.

Blend until smooth and creamy.

Add ice cubes and blend again until chilled.

Serve immediately.

Why it's great:
This smoothie is rich in protein from the powder and flaxseeds, while the strawberries add a refreshing sweetness. It's an antioxidant-rich, low-carb option for anyone looking for a refreshing, nutrient-packed drink.

## 20. Tropical Protein Shake

Prep Time: 5 minutes
Cook Time: 0 minutes
Servings: 1

### Ingredients:

1 scoop tropical-flavored protein powder

1/4 cup coconut milk

1/2 cup unsweetened almond milk

1/4 cup mango, diced

1/4 cup pineapple, diced

Ice cubes

### Instructions:

Add the tropical protein powder, coconut milk, almond milk, mango, pineapple, and ice cubes to a blender.

Blend until smooth and creamy.

Serve immediately.

Why it's great:
This tropical protein shake provides a refreshing, fruity taste, while the coconut and almond milk deliver healthy fats and a creamy texture. The mango and pineapple are rich in vitamins, making it a great drink for a nutrient-packed snack or post-workout recovery.

# Chapter 8: Meal Planning & Tips

### Creating a Balanced High-Protein, Low-Carb Meal Plan

When following a high-protein, low-carb diet, meal planning is essential for ensuring that your nutritional needs are met while keeping you on track with your health and fitness goals. A well-rounded meal plan should include a variety of high-protein foods, healthy fats, and low-carb vegetables, ensuring that your body receives all the nutrients it needs without unnecessary carbs.

### Here's how to create a balanced high-protein, low-carb meal plan:

### Prioritize Protein:
Protein is the cornerstone of this diet, so aim to include a good source of protein in every meal. This could include lean meats, poultry, fish, eggs, dairy, or plant-based protein sources like tofu, tempeh, and legumes.

Incorporate Healthy Fats:
Healthy fats are important for satiety and overall health. Include sources such as avocados, nuts, seeds, olive oil, and coconut oil in your meals. These fats help you feel fuller for longer while providing essential fatty acids.

### Focus on Low-Carb Vegetables:
Vegetables should make up a large portion of your meals. Choose non-starchy vegetables such as spinach, kale, broccoli, cauliflower, zucchini, and bell peppers. These are nutrient-dense, high in fibre, and low in carbs.

### Avoid Refined Carbs and Sugars:
Eliminate refined grains (like white bread, pasta, and rice) and sugary foods. Instead, opt for healthy, whole-food sources of carbohydrates, such as cauliflower rice, zucchini noodles, and sweet potatoes (in moderation).

### Plan for Snacks:
Include high-protein snacks such as hard-boiled eggs, Greek yogurt, cheese, nuts, or protein balls to keep you satisfied between meals and prevent overeating.

## Sample Weekly Meal Plan for Beginners

Here's a sample meal plan for a week, designed to be simple and beginner-friendly. Feel free to adjust portion sizes based on your specific needs and preferences.

### Day 1:

Breakfast: Scrambled eggs with spinach and avocado

Lunch: Grilled chicken breast with mixed greens and olive oil dressing

Dinner: Salmon with roasted cauliflower and broccoli

Snack: Almonds and a protein shake

### Day 2:

Breakfast: Greek yogurt with flaxseeds and chia seeds

Lunch: Turkey lettuce wraps with avocado, tomato, and mustard

Dinner: Beef stir-fry with zucchini noodles and bell peppers

Snack: Cheese and cucumber slices

### Day 3:

Breakfast: Protein smoothie with almond butter and banana

Lunch: Tuna salad with mixed greens, cucumber, and olive oil dressing

Dinner: Baked chicken thighs with roasted Brussels sprouts and a side of mashed cauliflower

Snack: Boiled eggs with a sprinkle of salt

**Day 4:**

Breakfast: Omelette with mushrooms, cheese, and avocado

Lunch: Grilled shrimp with mixed greens and a lemon vinaigrette

Dinner: Pork chops with sautéed spinach and a side of green beans

Snack: Greek yogurt with a handful of berries

**Day 5:**

Breakfast: Chia seed pudding with coconut milk and almonds

Lunch: Grilled steak with a side of roasted vegetables

Dinner: Zucchini lasagna with ground turkey and marinara sauce

Snack: Protein bar

**Day 6:**

Breakfast: Cottage cheese with cucumber slices and olive oil

Lunch: Grilled chicken with avocado, lettuce, and salsa wrapped in a low-carb tortilla

Dinner: Grilled shrimp skewers with cauliflower rice

Snack: Veggie sticks with hummus

**Day 7:**

Breakfast: Protein pancakes with sugar-free syrup

Lunch: Egg salad with avocado and a side of leafy greens

Dinner: Baked cod with roasted vegetables

Snack: Hard-boiled eggs with a handful of nuts

## Meal Prep Tips and Tricks for Time Efficiency

Meal prepping can save time and ensure that you stay on track with your diet throughout the week. Here are a few tips to make meal prep easier:

**Cook in Batches:**
Prepare large batches of protein (chicken, turkey, beef, etc.) and vegetables (roast several servings at once) to save time throughout the week. Store them in airtight containers for easy access.

**Use Slow Cookers or Instant Pots:**
These tools allow you to prepare meals with minimal effort. Simply add your protein, vegetables, and seasonings, and let the slow cooker or pressure cooker do the work while you focus on other tasks.

**Pre-Cut Vegetables:**

Chop or spiralize your vegetables in advance and store them in the fridge. This will save time when it's time to cook your meals.

**Prepare Snacks in Bulk:**
Pre-portion your snacks (like nuts, cheese, or protein balls) into small containers or bags so they're ready to grab and go.

**Store Meals in the Freezer:**
If you make extra servings, freeze them for a later time. This is especially useful for dishes like stews, soups, and casseroles that freeze well.

## How to Track Your Macros and Progress

Tracking your macros (protein, fat, and carbs) helps ensure you stay on track with your high-protein, low-carb diet. Here's how to do it:

**Use a Macro-Tracking App:**
Apps like MyFitnessPal or Cronometer allow you to easily input the foods you eat and track your protein, fat, and carb intake. Many of these apps have barcode scanners, making it simple to log packaged foods.

**Set Your Macro Goals:**
Your daily macros will depend on your personal goals (weight loss, muscle gain, maintenance). A general guideline is to aim for 40-50% protein, 30-40% fat, and 10-20% carbs, but this may vary depending on your needs.

**Weigh and Measure Your Food:**
To get an accurate sense of your portion sizes and macros, use a food scale and measuring cups. This ensures you're not over or underestimating your intake.

**Monitor Your Progress:**
In addition to tracking macros, keep an eye on your physical progress. Take regular measurements, photos, or track body composition changes. This will give you a more comprehensive view of how the diet is working for you.

**Understanding Macros: Protein, Fat, and Carbs**
To make the most out of your high-protein, low-carb diet, it's important to understand the role of each macronutrient:

**Protein:**
Protein is essential for muscle repair, recovery, and growth. It helps you feel full and supports fat loss by maintaining lean muscle mass. Aim to get a significant portion of your calories from high-quality protein sources like meat, fish, eggs, and dairy.

Fat:
Healthy fats are important for brain health, hormone regulation, and satiety. Include sources of unsaturated fats, such as avocado, olive oil, and nuts, in your meals. Fat also helps to slow the digestion of carbohydrates, making it easier to maintain steady energy levels.

**Carbs:**
Carbohydrates provide energy, but on a low-carb diet, you'll aim to keep carbs to a minimum to encourage fat-burning. Focus on non-starchy vegetables like leafy greens, broccoli, and cauliflower. Limit grains, legumes, and starchy vegetables.

## How to Measure Portion Sizes

Measuring your portion sizes ensures you stay within your desired calorie and macro ranges. Here are a few tips:

**Use a Food Scale:**
A food scale is the most accurate way to measure portions. Weigh your protein, vegetables, and other ingredients to get precise measurements.

**Use Measuring Cups and Spoons:**
For items like oils, nut butters, and liquids, measuring cups and spoons can help you stick to your portion sizes.

**Fist, Palm, and Thumb Method:**
As a quick guideline, use your fist for vegetables, your palm for protein, and your thumb for fats (like oils or nuts). This is a handy way to visually estimate portion sizes when you're on the go.

## Staying on Track with Your Goals

**Stay Consistent:**
The key to success is consistency. Stick to your meal plan, track your macros, and focus on nutrient-dense foods that align with your dietary goals.

**Have a Cheat Meal, Not a Cheat Day:**
If you have a craving or social event, allow yourself a cheat meal, but avoid going off track for the entire day. A single meal won't derail your progress if you get back on track right after.

**Plan Ahead for Challenges:**
When you know you'll be busy or in a situation where sticking to your diet is challenging, plan ahead. Pack your meals or snacks, and be prepared to make healthier choices when eating out.

## Practical Tips for Sticking to the Diet

**Keep Healthy Snacks Handy:**
Keep protein-rich, low-carb snacks with you to avoid temptation when hunger strikes. Examples include nuts, boiled eggs, and cheese sticks.

**Prepare for Social Situations:**
If you're going to a party or gathering, bring a dish you can enjoy. It's much easier to stick to your diet if you know you'll have something safe to eat.

**Find Accountability:**
Whether it's a workout partner, a coach, or an online community, having someone to check in with will help keep you motivated and accountable.

## The Importance of Hydration

Proper hydration is crucial on any diet, especially when following a high-protein, low-carb plan. Water helps with digestion, nutrient absorption, and supports overall well-being.

**Aim for 8-10 Glasses of Water:**
Drink plenty of water throughout the day to stay hydrated. The amount may vary based on activity levels and climate, but a general rule of thumb is 8-10 cups per day.

**Stay Hydrated with Electrolytes:**
When you reduce carbs, your body excretes more water and electrolytes. Consider adding a pinch of sea salt to your water or drinking an electrolyte-rich drink to maintain balance.

## Tips on Staying Hydrated and Supporting Fat Loss

**Drink Water Before Meals:**
Drinking water before meals helps with satiety, preventing overeating and supporting fat loss.

**Herbal Teas:**
Herbal teas, such as peppermint, ginger, or green tea, are hydrating and can aid digestion while providing a refreshing, low-calorie beverage.

**Infuse Your Water:**
If plain water isn't exciting enough, infuse it with fruits, herbs, or cucumber to add flavour without extra calories.

Meal planning, proper hydration, and tracking your macros are key to staying on track with your high-protein, low-carb goals. With these tips, you'll be well on your way to achieving your health and fitness objectives!

# Appendix

## Frequently Asked Questions (FAQ)

1. What is a high-protein, low-carb diet?
A high-protein, low-carb diet focuses on increasing protein intake while limiting the consumption of carbohydrates. The goal is to help with fat loss, muscle gain, and improving overall health by relying on protein as the main source of energy instead of carbohydrates.

2. How much protein should I eat on a high-protein, low-carb diet?
The amount of protein you should consume depends on your goals. A general guideline is to aim for 1.2-2.0 grams of protein per kilogram of body weight per day, especially if you are focusing on muscle gain or fat loss. For weight maintenance, the lower end of the range may be sufficient.

3. Are all carbs bad on a low-carb diet?
No, not all carbs are bad. On a low-carb diet, you should focus on non-starchy vegetables, fruits (in moderation), and low-carb whole grains (such as quinoa and oats in small amounts). Avoid refined carbs and processed foods high in sugar.

4. How can I make sure I'm getting enough nutrients on a low-carb diet?
To ensure you're getting the necessary nutrients, focus on a variety of protein sources, healthy fats, and low-carb vegetables. Incorporate foods rich in fibre, vitamins, and minerals like leafy greens, berries, nuts, and seeds.

5. Can I still eat out on a high-protein, low-carb diet?
Yes, dining out can still fit into your high-protein, low-carb diet. Opt for grilled, baked, or roasted meats, seafood, or salads with protein toppings. Avoid bread, pasta, and starchy sides, and ask for substitutions like extra vegetables or a side of avocado.

6. Can I drink alcohol on a high-protein, low-carb diet?
Alcoholic beverages like wine, whiskey, and clear spirits (such as vodka) are lower in carbs and can be consumed in moderation. However, avoid sugary cocktails or beer, as they tend to be higher in carbs.

7. How do I track my macros?
Tracking your macros involves logging your meals and the macronutrients (protein, fats, and carbs) they contain. You can use apps like MyFitnessPal or Cronometer to track your daily intake. Make sure to weigh your food and read labels to get accurate information.

8. Can I follow a high-protein, low-carb diet if I'm vegetarian or vegan?
Yes, it's entirely possible to follow a high-protein, low-carb diet as a vegetarian or vegan. Focus on plant-based protein sources like tofu, tempeh, lentils, seitan, edamame, and plant-based protein powders. Pair them with low-carb vegetables and healthy fats.

## Glossary of Key Terms

Macronutrients: The three main nutrients (protein, fat, and carbohydrates) that provide energy and are essential for bodily functions.

Protein: An essential macronutrient used for muscle repair, growth, and overall health. It's a key component in a high-protein diet.

Carbohydrates (Carbs): A macronutrient that provides energy. In a low-carb diet, the goal is to limit carb intake and focus on non-starchy vegetables and some fruits.

Ketosis: A metabolic state in which your body burns fat for fuel instead of carbohydrates. This state is commonly associated with low-carb diets and ketogenic diets.

Insulin Sensitivity: The body's ability to respond to insulin, the hormone that regulates blood sugar. A high-protein, low-carb diet can help improve insulin sensitivity.

Net Carbs: The total carbohydrates in a food minus the fibre content, as fibre does not affect blood sugar levels. When tracking carbs on a low-carb diet, many people focus on net carbs.

Macros: Short for macronutrients, the three primary types of nutrients that provide energy: protein, fat, and carbohydrates.

Caloric Deficit: A state where you consume fewer calories than your body burns, leading to weight loss. This is a common goal for many on a low-carb, high-protein diet.

Fats: A macronutrient that provides energy, supports cell function, and aids in the absorption of certain vitamins. Healthy fats like avocados, olive oil, and nuts are emphasized in low-carb diets.

## Conversion Table for UK & US Measurements

| Ingredient | UK Measurement | US Measurement |
|---|---|---|
| Water, Milk, Juice | 1 cup = 240 ml | 1 cup = 8 fl oz |
| Olive Oil | 1 tbsp = 15 ml | 1 tbsp = 0.5 fl oz |
| Almond Milk | 1 cup = 240 ml | 1 cup = 8 fl oz |
| Butter | 1 oz = 28.35 g | 1 oz = 1/4 cup |
| Cheese (Grated) | 1 oz = 28.35 g | 1 oz = 1/4 cup |
| Almond Flour | 1 cup = 96 g | 1 cup = 3.4 oz |
| Oven Temperature | 180°C | 350°F |
| 1 inch | 2.54 cm | 1 inch = 2.54 cm |
| 1 foot | 30.48 cm | 1 foot = 12 in |

## Resources & Recommended Tools

To help you succeed on your high-protein, low-carb journey, here are some useful resources and tools:

### Meal Planning Apps:

MyFitnessPal: Track calories and macros with ease.

Chronometer: A detailed app that tracks not only macros but also micronutrients.

Eat This Much: Automatically generates meal plans based on your nutritional goals.

### Kitchen Tools:

Food Scale: An essential tool for measuring portions and tracking macros.

Blender: Perfect for making smoothies, shakes, and protein-packed beverages.

Slow Cooker/Instant Pot: Ideal for easy meal prep, especially for meats and stews.

Meal Prep Containers: Store your prepared meals and snacks to ensure you stay on track during the week.

### Protein Powders:

Whey Protein: Ideal for those who tolerate dairy and seek fast absorption.

Plant-Based Protein: Perfect for vegetarians and vegans, made from peas, rice, hemp, or soy.

Collagen Protein: Supports joints, skin, and overall connective tissue health.

### Cookbooks:

The High-Protein, Low-Carb Cookbook by Louise Goss

The Keto Reset Diet by Mark Sisson

The 30-Minute Ketogenic Cooking by Rami Abrams

## Websites & Blogs:

Diet Doctor: Offers comprehensive guides, recipes, and meal plans for low-carb and keto diets.

Ruled.me: A popular website with tons of keto and low-carb recipes, along with meal plans and guides.

KetoConnect: A great resource for low-carb, high-protein recipes and meal prep tips.

## Fitness Trackers:

Fitbit: Helps you monitor your activity levels, calories burned, and progress.

Apple Watch: Tracks steps, heart rate, and overall activity, and syncs with meal-tracking apps.

This appendix provides everything you need to supplement your high-protein, low-carb lifestyle—from practical tips and tools to tracking macros and meal planning. Make sure to use these resources to stay organized, motivated, and on track with your health goals!

Printed in Dunstable, United Kingdom